The
Prose Works of Roberto Arlt:
A Thematic Approach

Jack M. Flint

UNIVERSITY OF DURHAM 1985

© Jack M. Flint 1985

ISBN 0 907310 09 5

HM4

$c\ ^{c}$

This book was produced using the word processing package WORD-STAR on a CIFER 2684 microcomputer running CP/M. The edited text was processed to convert WORDSTAR characters to standard ASCII characters, and then copied to floppy disc. This disc was then input into the MILES 33 word processor system by Titus Wilson and Son Ltd., paged automatically and output to a LINOTRON 202. It is set in PLANTIN.

304655

PRINTED FOR DURHAM MODERN LANGUAGES SERIES
BY
TITUS WILSON AND SON LTD.
28 HIGHGATE
KENDAL   CUMBRIA

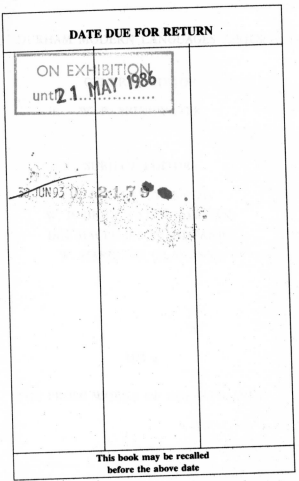

Table of Contents

Acknowledgements

I am indebted to Professor I. R. Macpherson for his help and advice and to Mrs Ann Whyatt for her care in preparing the text. I should also like to thank The British Academy for their generous offer of an award which has made this publication possible.

INTRODUCTION

Roberto Arlt has commanded attention from Argentine critics since Raúl Larra published his biographically-orientated work on him in 1950[1] and Nira Etchenique her slender study of 1962.[2] His death in July 1942 provoked a number of brief but worthwhile articles in journals and reviews[3] and there was a further efflorescence of interest in 1954.[4] Until the publication of Goštautas's work on him,[5] little or no criticism had emanated from outside Argentina. Since his death his name has been wielded in his native country by those who have claimed him as a champion in the anti-bourgeois and anti-intellectual cause, particularly during the troubled years in Argentine politics since 1945. He has been invoked more often as an iconoclast than as a novelist or playwright and his reputation has consequently risen and fallen with little regard for his abilities as a writer.

Later studies by Núñez,[6] Masotta[7] and Maldavsky[8] have gone some way towards setting this right but all suffer from a limited perspective, particularly Maldavsky's with its narrow neo-Freudian interpretations. With the exception of Goštautas, and more notably, Hayes's short study,[9] none of these works deals with Arlt as a novelist and prose writer in the widest sense and even with Goštautas, little attempt is made to come to terms with his technique in an analytical way. Numerous general assumptions have been made and he has been seized upon more as a man than as an author, suffering at the hands of his friends and foes alike. Arlt was a combative figure, living out his short and rather frantic existence (1900-42) during a vital period of development in Argentina and, more importantly, in Buenos Aires. It is not possible to understand him fully without reference to the development of *porteño* society during his formative and productive years from 1916 onwards and we shall be obliged to establish certain parallels in this respect. But it is unjust to invoke him for what he was rather than award him his place in Argentine literature for what he wrote. That he has an important place is now beyond doubt, for not only did the late 1920s and the following decade witness the gestation of the modern Argentine novel as we now know it but Arlt himself may be seen to have contributed in a major way to the emergence of a new technique and also of a new life-view which was to be reflected in many later novelists. Carlos Mastronardi calls him "un admirable y arriesgado innovador", adding:

> Visto desde nuestro convulsivo presente, tan pródigo en creaciones destinadas a exaltar lo que hay de absurdo en toda existencia, cabe admitir que su

gravitación local, de día en día más notoria y firme, es la de un verdadero precursor.[10]

It will be our task in this study of his work to evaluate such opinion, to see Arlt against the disturbed times in which he wrote, to analyse his ideology and technique and to avoid as far as possible the dangers inherent in viewing Arlt the man at the expense of Arlt the writer.

Arlt began the composition of his major works in 1919.[11] His novels were published between 1926 and 1932. By 1931 he had already turned to the theatre with an adaptation of *Los siete locos* entitled *El humillado*, put on at the Teatro del Pueblo at the instance of his friend Leónidas Barletta, its founder and director.[12] He continued to write short stories and his *Aguafuertes* after his début in the theatre but his main interest had now shifted away from the novel. He remained active in the theatre until his death in 1942. Born at the turn of the century, he lived through a period of intense change in Buenos Aires which, with minor exceptions, formed the exclusive background to his life and works. Guillermo Ara writes of this important moment in Argentine literary history:

> Estamos ya en la década que va del 20 al 30, límite histórico que inicia un arduo y sostenido examen de la realidad argentina, ya liquidadas muchas ilusiones. La novela no se conforma con ser puramente expositiva; procura un esclarecimiento de la crisis política y moral que angustia al hombre. Eduardo Mallea y Roberto Arlt escrutan –desde ángulos muy diversos– la intimidad del hombre y su destino sudamericano.[13]

It is not within our brief to examine in a detailed fashion the political, social and philosophical upheaval which took place in Argentina at this time but some reference to it is essential for an understanding of Arlt's contribution to his age and an assessment of what he in his turn derived from his circumstances.

The years of 1916-40 were an epoch of great stress and structural change in Argentine society. They lead to a sharpening of what has come to be called the "crisis of identity" which is manifest not only in Arlt, with his themes of alienation and *desarraigo*, but in most of his contemporaries also. In Scalabrini Ortiz's *El hombre que está solo y espera* (1931), a significant title in itself, the same preoccupations are present. They are fundamental in Mallea's writing, whose isolated characters are in constant and fruitless search for self-affirmation and communication. They are to be found in the Gálvez of the thirties, particularly in *Hombres en soledad*, in which he veers away from his earlier social realism towards more metaphysical themes and accompanies Mallea in his exploration of the corrosive loneliness of Buenos Aires society.[14] They re-emerge in a host of later writers, amongst whom Sábato and Córtazar are perhaps best known outside their native Argentina. As Julio Mafud says in his penetrating analysis of Argentine society and culture:

Nunca los héroes argentinos encuentran o descubren el vínculo que los ubique en la convivencia social; este hecho los identifica. La sociedad se resiste por todos los medios a aceptarlos. Su primera actitud es de exclusión. La segunda, de rechazo. Arraigarse, afincarse, quedarse en algún punto remoto, en algún lugar ansiado, les está vedado. Para el héroe argentino todas las metas que conducen a la sociedad están dinamitadas.[15]

Mafud goes so far as to affirm that in this sense there is little to choose between Arlt's Erdosain and Mallea's Chaves, whom he sees as both from the same mould. "Son los que se han aislado convergiendo hacia sí mismos después que han sido excluidos desde afuera. El mundo de cada uno de estos personajes es cíclico; comienza y termina en su propio yo."

It is not necessary here to enter into the growth of this problem from a sociological point of view. It is sufficient to mention the massive immigration (preponderantly of Italians) into Argentina beginning towards the end of the last century,[16] the undeniable influence of the *pampa* on Argentine demographic distribution –"aquel mundo unilateralmente cronológico" Raimundo Lazo has called it–, the population explosion of the megapolis of Buenos Aires at the expense of rural life and the consequent sense of oppression in an overcrowded city, with immigrants crushed into the *conventillos* (slum tenements) and the concomitant social evils to which this gave rise.[17] To quote a detail from Tulio Carella, writing about the year of the Centenario (1910), when Arlt was on the threshold of adolescence:

El fabuloso crecimiento de la ciudad hizo rápidamente centro de lo que era arrabal; con todo, en el centro de antes, a pocos metros de la Casa Rosada y del Congreso, era posible encontrar cualquier tipo de casa de diversión y llegar a ella con los ojos cerrados, teniendo como guía el barullo y el olor.[18]

Facts and figures quoted by Carella about the infamous *trata de blancas* and the proliferation of prostitution make horrific if fascinating reading. (We shall have occasion to consider these later when we examine manifestations of this problem in Arlt's novels.) He calls the Buenos Aires of this period "una sociedad falocrática" – an apt phrase.

These years also saw the culmination of a process of brisk change in philosophical values in Argentina and in Latin America at large. Weakened by a rapidly deteriorating economic situation from 1916 onwards,[19] due to the effects of the first World War on Argentine trade and the political changes occurring in 1916, the influence of positivism finally declined. As Stabb points out in his careful analysis of this question, the attack on scientism had begun long before but it assumed landslide proportions by 1920. "Stated in very general terms" he says, "this ideological revolt was directed against the view of human affairs which holds that the totality of man's existence may be empirically analyzed and understood. Under attack was the corollary idea that the individual and society may be technologically manipulated. The revolutionaries, by contrast, affirmed that human affairs are highly problematical, that they are suffused with contingency and the unpredictable, that the rational-scientific approach to the world of nature has only limited value in explaining the human condition".[20] In its turn the philosophical landslide brought other institutions tumbling with it. 1918 saw the great university reform movement (subsequently so abortive) launched in Córdoba and spread through Latin America. In political affairs, Hipólito Irigoyen had assumed office as Radical President in 1916 and soon became a father figure for the middle classes and the underprivileged alike. As Romero put it, with Irigoyen "...el Estado dejó de ser sentido como algo fatalmente hostil y se abrió como una esperanza que, por cierto, no fue defraudada del todo".[21] These hopes and aspirations were to have their effect on artistic life, too, and the mid-twenties saw the emergence of the opposing groups of Florida and Boedo with their respective insistence on *el arte por el arte* (Florida) and a new feeling for social realism with the Russian masters as their mentors (Boedo). We shall examine Arlt's relationships with these two groups at the appropriate moment.

Understandably, therefore, as a new view of man and his society began to be forged, the younger writers and thinkers struck out for fresh fields for their creativity and enquiry. As the security of the old system of ideas was shattered, a new feeling for man and the contingency of his circumstances was born and an existential world-view was substituted for the absolutes of certainty and predictability which had held sway for so long. As Arlt's character, el Astrólogo, was to say in *Los lanzallamas* in 1931:

> Los hombres han perdido la costumbre de mirar las estrellas. Incluso, si se examinan sus vidas, se llega a la conclusión de que viven de dos maneras: Unos falseando el conocimiento de la verdad y otros aplastando la verdad. ... ¿Qué es la Verdad? me dirá usted. La verdad es el Hombre. El Hombre con su cuerpo. Los intelectuales, despreciando el cuerpo, han dicho: Busquemos la verdad, y verdad la llaman a especular sobre abstracciones. Se han escrito libros sobre todas las cosas. Incluso sobre la psicología del que mira volar un mosquito. [NCC II, 21].[22]

It would be idle to claim that this process was in any way peculiar to Argentina. The existentialist revolution was already afoot in Germany. But what is now well recognized is that the dissemination of European existential thought, helped in part by Ortega y Gasset during his first visit to Buenos Aires in 1916 and continued by native thinkers like Carlos Astrada, returning later from Germany, was more readily achieved in Argentina than elsewhere in Latin America and had its impact on literary creativity even before it made itself felt in Europe. In the novel, Arlt's existential revolt and Mallea's exploitation of the themes of anguish and solitude antedate the direction taken much later by the French novel. Argentina was rich ground for doctrines proclaiming the lonely condition of the individual in a hostile world. The theme of *soledad* may be held to be inherent in Argentine thinking and writing, albeit in a latent fashion. It was already apparent as far back as 1872, when Hernández published his *Martín Fierro*, a classic case of "outsider" literature. As Jean Franco says: "In plot, structure, language and metaphor, the poem extends beyond the regional to become universal myth – that of man's solitude".[23] We have already alluded to the social conditions and development that make solitude a central theme in Argentine literature: rootless immigration, the vast *pampa* and the breakneck growth of the "cabeza de Goliath", as Martínez Estrada called Buenos Aires. In the 1920s, therefore, there comes about a confluence of two streams of thought: the existential view of man inherent in the new feeling and the deep-rooted Argentine preoccupation with *soledad* and the individual's hopelessness when confronted by his hostile environment. In this way, the stage was set for the emergence of the modern –one is tempted to say the *true*– Argentine novel, with its insistence on the fallibility of reason, the lonely existence of man (and more particularly, of woman in the case of writers like Mallea), his irrationality, his anguish and the contingency of his circumstances. The mould of the contemporary Argentine novel was fashioned during this period; it has yet to be broken. The themes which manifested themselves in the 1920s with Arlt and his contemporaries were to be abiding ones. In Mallea, they give rise to impressive figures like Agata Cruz in *Todo verdor perecerá*, barren, anguished, separated from the world of her husband and that of mankind at large; in Arlt, to the suffering of an Erdosain, destroyed by his upbringing and his despair at his inability to discover some bedrock in his own existence, cut off from God, from Man and ultimately from the whole world, victim of a devouring city and of his own madness. At a later date, in Sábato's *Sobre héroes y tumbas*, they produce the elusive figure of Alejandra, persecuted by the madness in her family and her perverse relationship with her father, incapable of a fruitful contact with the one person who might save her and Castel, in Sábato's *El túnel*, urged forward by his own fallible reason to murder and to his doom. At the heart of all these characters is a fear of their own solitude and their unfulfilled desire to know not only themselves but their condition as human beings. As Mafud says: "Si hay una constante dominante, absoluta, en la literatura argentina, es, sin duda, y de un modo arquetípico, la imposibilidad de captar o asir la realidad que nos circunvala".[24]

Such then is the atmosphere that pervades Arlt's adolescent and later years from 1910 onwards, an atmosphere which he was to probe and expound in his novels and stories. Not, like Mallea, relying on an integrated system of philosophical ideas and values, but as one who lived and died from it, irrationally, painfully, often humorously, absorbing it and spewing it out in an undigested mass; fascinated, fearful, himself anguished, living out his own characters' lives, intuitively aware of the impossible aspirations that lurked in himself and in his fellow-men.

The need for additional understanding of the theme of alienation and solitude in the context of the Argentine novel is therefore clear, for, although it never came to occupy the formal position in Arlt's ideology that it does, say, with Mallea, it nevertheless constitutes a pervasive background to everything he wrote. It would not be a useful exercise in this short study to trace in a detailed manner the origins of loneliness in society. This is best left to the sociologist.[25] It is however instructive to review the thinking on this question of one or two of Arlt's contemporaries and subsequent writers, in order to set Arlt's exploitation of the theme in a wider framework. We have already mentioned Scalabrini Ortiz's *El hombre que está solo y espera*, published in 1931; that is, exactly at the time that Arlt was composing his mature novels. Scalabrini will therefore allow us to see what was in the air. In his work, the process of irrationality (or, more to the point, anti-rationality) is seen vividly at work. Moreover, since he is primarily concerned with the character of the *porteño* ("el Hombre de Corrientes y Esmeralda", as he calls him, these two being central streets in Buenos Aires), he provides us with an effective key for the understanding of Arlt's attitudes, as these were revealed in novelized form. In Scalabrini, the disenthronement of reason is paramount from the start. Alejandro Korn's declarations against "la pesadilla del automatismo mecánico" and Mallea's later attack on "los desiertos positivista y racionalista" find full echo here. "Atreverse a erigir en creencia los sentimientos arraigados en cada uno, por mucho que contraríen la rutina de creencias extintas, he allí todo el arte de la vida," writes Scalabrini.[26] In 1931, he conceived of American man as being essentially different from European man, the one being "individualista" and the other "mutualista", in his terms. The impact of the hostile and lonely city on the latter as an immigrant was to destroy him, thrusting him into a totally alien world. "El europeo, agobiado por la soledad, se volvió reservado, meditabundo. Hostigado por la inhumana temperancia, se encerró en sí mismo, sin más relación externa que la de algunos camaradas tan flagelados como él".[27] Scalabrini draws an important distinction between those *porteños* who were beyond fifty at that time and younger men. The former, according to his argument, had been moulded in a less rigid society, believing that science would conquer all. They built and were confident. But "en su obstinación mecánica y geométrica se olvidaron del hombre". (Arlt refers continually to "esta sociedad mecánica".) The younger *porteño*, however, is a misanthrope who hates his own solitude, who talks endlessly but is always lonely. "Soltero o casado, el Hombre de Corrientes y Esmeralda es un hombre que está

desnudo y solo en el interior de su escéptico baluarte verbal, que está
solo entre dos millones de hombres que están solos."[28] Compare Arlt's
protagonist Erdosain who is described as "absolutamente solo entre tres
mil millones de hombres y en el corazón de la ciudad" [NCC II, 34].
Returning to the anti-rational theme, Scalabrini maintains that "...en el
caos inextricable de la vida porteña, la inteligencia es incapaz de soluciones.
Solamente el arrojo del instinto induce probabilidades y propicia rutas."
Of course, he is also a convinced geographical determinist and he pushes
his arguments to the farthest limits. Thus he sees the *porteño*, although an
urban creature, as conforming to the very nature of the land: ..."pampa
llana sin mojones para la inteligencia y ... la vida de la ciudad que avanza
de azar en azar".[29]

A more recent commentator on this theme, also a convinced determinist,
is Héctor Murena, who identifies the same problem in Argentine national
life, referring to "esta sociedad de separados". Tracing the history of the
nation and its lack of agglutination as a society, he claims to discern that
soledad is the fundamental quality that distinguishes Argentina from other
nations and, as such, must be the predominant theme in its literature if
the writer is to be in touch with truly national traits.[30] According to
Murena, the problem has its roots not only in history but in the topographi-
cal loneliness of the *pampa* and "este monstruoso río, con su dilatado e
inerte cuerpo negador del movimiento"; the same river that Mallea too
had qualified as "el río inmóvil". "Aquí se da el caso" writes Murena,
"de un pueblo entero sumido en una soledad sin escapatorias, ante le
que se pueden ensayar todas las defensas pero que nadie elude, porque
justamente se impone como la anulación de las libertades personales,
porque es como una condena".[31] A reading of Mallea's novels and stories
of the 1930s and 1940s would lend full support to Murena's thesis,
although it is significant that Mallea raises the concept of the isolated
individual to much more universal levels.

Arlt's mature novels also belong to that period between 1929 and 1932
when the Western world was engulfed in an economic crisis of the gravest
proportions. Particularly serious were the effects in Argentina, giving rise
to conditions which led to the military coup of 1930, since when she has
never fully recovered her economic or political stability. Whilst it would
be hazardous to subscribe entirely to Adolfo Prieto's rather narrow view
of Arlt, he is correct in drawing attention to this conjunction of circumstances. As he writes, *"Los siete locos* (1929) será el exacto correlato
novelístico de una sociedad desquiciada en sus bases económicas".[32] If
this, and only this, were true of Arlt's work, then it would be a mere social
document to which we might turn for an understanding of the internal
workings of Buenos Aires society during this period. But what Goštautas
has called "la penosa impresión de tristeza y angustia que abruma a los

personajes y al lector" has its origins in more fundamental and universal causes which make Arlt worthy of our wider attention.[33]

This is the atmosphere of social and philosophical reappraisal which Arlt imbibes, not perhaps as a conscious student, for he had little or no formal education, but as a typical *porteño*; an atmosphere from which the canons of safe, positivist thinking had been banished without there having arisen any firm attitude to replace them. It is to the emergence of this new attitude that Arlt contributed with his major novels *Los siete locos* and *Los lanzallamas* and his numerous short stories, consciously or unconsciously designed to highlight the contingency and loneliness of life in the great city of Buenos Aires and, on a higher plane, the anguish of modern man, trapped and strangled by forces, both external and psychological, which he neither understands nor is able to control. As Etchenique says: "Arlt trae el soplo vivo de la ciudad y lo trae no como escenario para la ubicación geográfica de su novela, sino como esencia y médula de su literatura".[34] When to this feeling is added his discovery of Dostoevsky during the early 1920s, and a compulsive interest in deviant psychology, it is not difficult to appreciate the genesis of his anguished novels. Those who have discovered in Arlt a systematic revolutionary attack on society are surely mistaken. When Raúl Larra says, for example, "...casi toda su obra está empapada de un espíritu de crítica social –que debemos recoger– y de un tono de desesperación, que debemos rechazar", he is not grasping the nettle.[35] Whilst it would be wrong to gainsay the importance of Arlt's invective against society throughout these works, what lives, and will live, is rather the cry of anguish and despair which his characters utter, not merely the social criticism or the sombre humour of the proposals for the obliteration of society by violence and plague or the financing of the revolution by a chain of brothels. Arlt was in oblivion for many years and deliberately ignored by the more aesthetic circles in Argentine life. What now commands our attention is not what he proposed –there are no real propositions in his work– but his prophetic realization that something was wrong with the kind of society that was being forged during the 1920s and his intuition and comprehension of the desperation of urban man manipulated by social and technological forces in an adverse and dehumanizing environment. As Luis Harss says of him: "Desde Arlt, que dio la primera cachetada metafísica, la novela del Río de la Plata ha vivido cada vez más a las patadas con la vida cotidiana".[36] Arlt was uttering a "cri de coeur" which put him well ahead of his times. Whilst many a modern reader will be unmoved by what is circumstantial in his writing, like his insistence on gas warfare, which mars parts of *Los lanzallamas*, he will not easily refuse to listen to Arlt's voice of despair and anguish and his vibrant feeling for life – a life which he realized some fifty years ago had already taken a turn for the worse. "Yo creo que Dios es la alegría de vivir", cries the young Silvio in *El juguete rabioso*. "La horrible miseria está en nosotros, es la miseria de adentro ... del alma que nos cala los huesos como la sífilis", says Erdosain in *Los siete locos*. Between these two extremes lies the question we must now unravel.

CHAPTER I

THE CONCEPT OF ANGUISH

Arlt makes no coherent exposition of his philosophy. The introspective pleasures of the writer's journal were not for him, faced by the need to wage a daily struggle for existence. What affirmations he makes about himself are grossly unreliable and highly imaginative and sometimes even false where personal details are concerned. His good friend Roberto Mariani once wrote:

> Se me ocurre imaginar qué desastroso retrato personal de Roberto Arlt haría el futuro historiador de la literatura argentina cuando, componiendo su librote, y precediendo al juicio estrictamente crítico, utilizase esos "documentos humanos" de primera mano, esas confesiones directas del mismo Roberto Arlt, dándole plena fe...[1]

We must therefore proceed with caution from Arlt's statements to the works themselves, for no trustworthy correlation exists. In general, we shall prefer to deduce his ideology from the writings he has left behind, although we shall clearly be obliged to refer now and then to his pugnacious affirmations about his own and other author's work. Arlt's thinking is anarchic and unsystematic, springing more from a "gut reaction" to his life and times than from any aprioristic reasoning. This makes our task somewhat hazardous since the areas of thought that we shall try to define in his writing often overlap and interpenetrate.[2] Having made this caveat, let us cautiously listen to Arlt speaking about himself:

> ¿Qué opino de mí mismo? Que soy un individuo inquieto y angustiado por este permanente problema: de qué modo debe vivir el hombre para ser feliz, o mejor dicho, de qué modo debía vivir yo para ser completamente dichoso.
>
> Como uno no puede hacer de su vida un laboratorio de ensayos por la falta de tiempo, dinero y cultura, desdoblo de mis deseos personajes imaginarios que trato de novelar.[3]

Later in the same statement, he goes on to say: "Soy un perfecto egoísta. La felicidad del hombre y de la humanidad no me interesa un pepino". Typically enough, not only are the two parts of this self-judgment at variance but the basic premise is patently untrue. Arlt *is* interested, if not in man's happiness, then certainly in his unhappiness and his despair.

The origin of the theme of anguish in Arlt's thinking therefore demands elucidation at this stage before we examine its ramifications in his creative writing. Not only does it point the way towards the new view of man which was beginning to fill the vacuum left by the decay of positivism but, in passing, it will allow us to consider his relationship with the major tendencies of the period in Argentina, embodied in the Florida/Boedo dispute. It is significant that Mallea and Arlt, the two important figures who were to become dominant in the novel of the late twenties and early thirties in Argentina, as subsequent criticism has shown, contrived in each case to avoid being absorbed into this doctrinal literary controversy. Each in his own way elevates the scrutiny of the individual in his loneliness and anguish into the prime consideration of his work and marries the problem of form and renovation of expression (characteristic of Florida) with the search for a social content which might provide new directions in prose-writing (Boedo). Numerous attempts have been made to place Arlt in one camp or the other, particularly in Boedo. Barletta states that he remained neutral until 1929, "...el año en que se radicó definitivamente en Boedo".[4] Arlt himself lends credence to this view when he says: "En el grupo llamado de Boedo encontramos a Castelnuovo, Mariani, yo y Barletta. La característica de este grupo sería *un interés por el sufrimiento humano*, su desprecio por el arte de quincalla...".[5] Larra maintains that "Arlt, sin participar para nada en la polémica, mantiene vinculación personal con ambos grupos".[6] Goštautas, writing more recently, claims: "Habría que colocar a Arlt dentro del grupo de los independientes, como lo fue Horacio Quiroga".[7] It is not appropriate for us to examine the dispute in detail but a brief outline will enable us to savour the general atmosphere in which Arlt's first literary steps were taken and to see something of the genesis of his major themes.

The polemic came to a head in 1925. It centred on two rival *cenáculos*, that of the popular Boedo (a street lying outside the centre of Buenos Aires) and that of Florida, the fashionable and elegant central street, where the *artepuristas* met to share their theories and writing. Alvaro Yunque lends colour to the controversy:

> Florida era el centro de Buenos Aires, la vía de las grandes tiendas, la del lujo exquisito, la cantada por Darío con profusión de oros y palabras bellas, la calle donde está el Jockey Club y donde una clase social –y sus acólitos– exhibía su cotidiano ocio. ...Boedo era el surburbio chato y gris, calle de boliches, de cafetines y teatrejos refugio del dominical cansancio obrero, calle que nunca tuvo poeta que la cantara, calle cosmopolita, ruidosa, de futboliers, guaranga, amenazante. Florida tenía pasado, tradición porteña. Boedo era lo gringo, lo importado, lo actual.[8]

A popular tango of the time celebrated Boedo in more picturesque terms:

> Barrio de hacha y tiza, papuso, canyengue,
> ande tuvo cuna la nueva emoción,
> ande el alma rea sigue usando lengue
> y el tango se tuerce como un bandoneón.[9]

The principal organs through which the rival groups disseminated their respective ideologies were *Claridad* (Boedo), named after Barbusse's left-wing publication in Paris, *Clarté*, and *Martín Fierro* (Florida), redolent by its very title of *criollo* traditions.[10] Florida argued for art for art's sake, Boedo for social realism. Florida was *vanguardista*, Boedo anarchist and socialist. More important for our present purposes were the external influences upon them. Florida had its eyes on Western Europe, particularly France, in the hope of effecting a renewal in Argentine literary values, taking its inspiration from the French avant-garde of the early post-war period. Boedo, inflamed by the success of the Russian Revolution in 1917, turned to Kropotkin, Bakunin and Marx as its ideologues and to Tolstoy and Dostoevsky as its literary masters and to a lesser degree Andreyev, Gorky and Gogol. In a sense, bitter though it was, the dispute was more important for the reawakening that it brought to Argentine (and particularly Buenos Aires) literature and for the creation of a more avid reading public than for any outstanding work that it produced in either of the rival camps. As Dardo Cúneo rightly asks: "¿Lo necesario, rigurosa-mente necesario de una vez por todas, es emplazar en alta voz: ¿Dónde está la obra perdurable de Florida como Florida y de Boedo como Boedo?".[11]

Perhaps for temperamental reasons, Arlt held himself aloof from the controversy for a long time, refusing to subscribe to the purely social themes held in favour by Boedo and sustaining his interest in a renewal of literary form. In spite of his remarks quoted above, it is difficult to ascribe him in a categorical way to the Boedo faction. His daughter, Mirta Arlt, feels that he must be placed "espiritualmente" with Boedo. Adolfo Prieto is more acute in his summing-up. "El individualismo anárquico de Arlt, su odio a los cenáculos, y el carácter de su novelística (angustia, violencia, irracionalismo), lo apartan tan naturalmente de Florida como de Boedo, y aun de las coordenadas generales que imprimen cierta unidad a la literatura de esos años."[12] What is more significant is that by 1926, when Arlt finished the composition of his first novel, a full-scale literary polemic was raging in Buenos Aires, creating a new sensitivity in writer and public alike, new directions of enquiry for the novel and new themes for exploration. For Arlt, the new direction was to be away from traditional Argentine themes towards an existential study of the urban individual. The key to that study was to be his concept of anguish.

By his own account, he wrote *El juguete rabioso* between 1919 and 1926, but, on analysis, it seems likely that the youthful part of its composition relates only to the first long chapter and that the subsequent chapters (II, III and IV) are the product of the middle twenties, so brusque is the change of tone from adolescent reminiscences and picaresque adventure to adult awareness. The theme of anguish makes its first incursion at the beginning of Chapter II, when the philosophical key is abruptly modulated. Hitherto, the work had been concerned with the simple adventures of the "Caballeros de la Medianoche" (a group of young adolescents), their nocturnal thefts, pursuit by the police and similar vicissitudes. Suddenly, the tone of anguish, which was to remain a constant in Arlt's adult writing, takes hold of the novel. The likeliest explanation for this unevenness is not so much the delay in composition as the fact that Arlt's desperate view of life, not to mention his early family experience, which was precarious and unhappy, had come upon a ready model for its expression. That model was, in all probability, the Russian master, only recently "discovered" by his contemporaries in Boedo, – Dostoevsky. That he was by now familiar with the Russian's works is not too difficult to show, as we shall see. An obvious clue to this relationship would seem to lie in the sudden intrusion into the novel of the perverse, gratuitous act of treachery with which he chose to end the work, which clearly has its ancestry in Dostoevsky.[13] It is contemporaneous with Gide's adaptation of the *acte gratuit* into the French novel, with the famous Lafcadio incident in *Les Caves du Vatican*,[14] and foreshadows the importance that the phenomenon was later to assume with the French existentialists. As Juan Carlos Ghiano says, "su [Arlt's] descubrimiento de los novelistas rusos ... le enseñó que las rutas más complicadas y atractivas están en las conciencias, no en los accidentes y sorpresas de tierras y mares".[15] Until the discovery of the theme of anguish as the driving force of his writing, Arlt's narrative was showing signs of becoming a mere string of adventures, culled from his youthful reading of *folletines*. With the explosion of anguish in *El juguete*, his new direction was assured. Goštautas has adequately laid the ghost concerning the disputed influence of Dostoevsky,[16] a matter we shall analyse further in due course. But before doing so, it is necessary to trace the evolution of the theme of suffering and anguish in the novels and the closely related concept of humiliation and self-abasement, in which it is also possible to demonstrate Arlt's close kinship with his Russian mentor.

A cursory reading of Arlt's novels might suggest that he was at pains to reveal every dirty corner of man's existence; his material greed, his sexual perverseness, his destructive and homicidal tendencies, his religious and political gullibility. But beneath the repulsive surface of this apparent view of mankind there vibrates a different life, a world in which the characters aspire to saintliness and purity, to self-sacrifice, sometimes even to the sacrifice of others in their drive towards an elusive happiness. It is in the contradiction between these two worlds, between man's aspirations and his base condition in society, that the anguish of Erdosain, Hipólita and the rest is generated. It is the first premise of all of Arlt's writing that man is born to suffering. "Es que llevamos el sufrimiento en nosotros. Una vez llegué a pensar" says Erdosain, "que flotaba en el aire ... era una idea ridícula; pero lo cierto es que la disconformidad está en uno" [NCC I 344]. As Mastronardi says of him: "Encontramos en Arlt ... un definido modo de reaccionar ante el mundo y una personalísima visión de la existencia. Tiende a decirnos que el sufrimiento es condición de todos, hasta de aquéllos que por haber caído muy bajo parecen escindidos del género humano".[17] For Arlt, man's destiny is sombre beyond belief. Victim of a cosmic loneliness, he is separated from God and his fellow man, "solo entre tres mil millones de hombres." "Donde vayas irá contigo la desesperación," Erdosain claims to himself. "Sufrirás y dirás como ahora: 'Más lejos todavía', y no hay más lejos sobre la tierra. El más lejos no existe. No existió nunca. Verás tristeza adonde vayas" [NCC II 56]. He is steadfastly convinced of his fate in spite of every measure he takes to palliate it. In spite of his search for love, carnal and spiritual, in spite of his revolt, all his aspirations to purity and happiness are doomed from the start. "...no estuvo en mis manos el ser un hombre bueno. Otras fuerzas oscuras me torcieron ... me tiraron abajo" [NCC I 338]. But the problem goes beyond, is greater than, the individual, for suffering in Arlt's view is a universal phenomenon, which leads him into the bitterest comments on human destiny. "En vez de felicitarnos del nacimiento de una criatura", he writes in his short story 'El jorobadito', "debíamos llorar de haber provocado la aparición en este mundo de un mísero y débil cuerpo humano, que a través de los años sufrirá incontables horas de dolor y escasísimos minutos de alegría" [NCC III 213].

Although suffering and anguish are therefore seen as an unavoidable concomitant of man's existence, it is nonetheless possible to distinguish their genesis in certain characters, especially in Erdosain, in given circumstances. We are now moving on to shifting sands, for quite naturally Arlt not only refrains in most cases from offering a well-founded or logical basis for their condition (they are, after all, seven *madmen*) but such evidence as is adduced is deliberately garbled and chronologically scrambled. For example, the childhood psychological reasons for Erdosain's sense of humiliation are concealed until well into *Los lanzallamas* and the reader of *Los siete locos* is expected to accept his condition quite blandly, without question or enquiry. In order to introduce some measure of order into this deliberate chaos for the purpose of analysis (this is not to criticize the chaos that Arlt purposely introduces in his novels, in which there *is* considerable "order", as we hope to demonstrate later) we shall discuss the origin of anguish in his characters under the following somewhat arbitrary headings: metaphysical speculations; the impact of technology and technological society on the individual; sexual and psychological reasons. We shall then consider the associated concept of humiliation and the antidotes that the characters adopt, in vain, and as we proceed we shall see to what extent many of these concepts may be traced back to Dostoevsky's undoubted influence.

Metaphysical anguish

Whilst we shall have occasion to note that many of the characters enjoy peculiar personal circumstances that render them vulnerable to life and provide a psychological motivation for their alienation and frustration, nevertheless, as human creatures, they all share in the common lack of fulfilment which has its roots in a metaphysical anguish born of their remoteness from the absolutes of purity and saintliness to which they aspire; their remoteness from God, as Arlt would put it. Throughout these novels, God is silent and removed. The awesome personal God of the Bible has been transformed by man in his urban surroundings into a useless and sterile God and here arises the first source of anguish. A large part of the disquisitions of the revolutionaries at the Astrólogo's house, which form the virtual backbone of these novels, concerns not revolution at all but the need to plug this metaphysical gap in man's existence, leading to blasphemous and amusing conclusions. Even as early as *El juguete rabioso*, as we have noted, metaphysical anguish erupts, almost without warning, in a sudden, disconcerting authorial intervention wedged into the otherwise picaresque progress of the book.

> Algunas veces en la noche.–Piedad, quién tendrá piedad de nosotros.
> Sobre esta tierra quién tendrá piedad de nosotros.
> Míseros, no tenemos un Dios ante quien postrarnos y toda nuestra pobre vida llora.
> ¿Ante quién me postraré, a quién hablaré de mis espinas y de mis zarzas duras, de este dolor que surgió en la tarde ardiente y que aún es en mí?
> Qué pequeñitos somos, y la madre tierra no nos quiso en sus brazos y henos aquí acerbos, desmantelados de impotencia.
> ¿Por qué no sabemos de nuestro Dios? [NCC I 139]

This anguished tone, totally absent from the earlier part of *El juguete rabioso*, foreshadows the shattering desperation which will take hold of Erdosain in the subsequent novels, as though Arlt had suddenly glimpsed the path he must pursue. Towards the end of *Los siete locos*, the same theme is taken up once more, amplified now to embrace the suffering of all mankind, a favourite concept with Mallea, incidentally.[18]

> No sufría por él, el hombre inscripto con un nombre en el registro civil, sino que su conciencia, apartándose del cuerpo, lo miraba como al de un extraño, y se decía: ¿Quién tendrá piedad del hombre?
> Y estas palabras, que acertaba a recoger su pensamiento, lo turbaban llenándolo de dolorosa ternura por invisibles prójimos. [NCC I 368]

Thus it is, claims Arlt, that the day will come when men will make revolution because they *need* a God. "Los hombres se declararán en huelga hasta que Dios no se haga presente" [NCC I 369]. Indeed, there are times in these novels when God is invested with an almost wilful sense of remoteness as though He, and not man, had fallen from grace.

A significant sequence is set in motion in *Los lanzallamas* when Erdosain witnesses a cat appealing to be allowed through a door. On this trivial incident, Arlt builds a whole metaphysical speculation about man's cosmic loneliness and suffering which borders on the blasphemous. The individual releasing the door becomes God and the cat provides an analogy for man. The passage must be quoted in full for the thought it contains lies at the centre of Arlt's deliberations:

> El gato ha lanzado su S.O.S. y el hombre ha esperado tras la puerta. Realizó varios actos. Uno, inclinarse. Dos, acariciarlo en la espalda. Tres, pasarle la mano bajo el vientre. Cuatro, levantarlo. Pero ¿a mí? ¿A ellos? ¿A nosotros? Sí, a nosotros, Dios canalla. A nosotros. Te hemos llamado y no has venido. Se detiene y piensa: ¡Qué dulce palabra!
> –Lo hemos llamado y no ha venido. Lo hemos lla...ma...do...y no...ha...ve ...nido. Dulzura única. Lo hemos llamado y no ha venido. Podremos contestar así algún día: "Nosotros lo llamamos y El no vino". Erdosain cierra los ojos. Deja que un intervalo de oscuridad penetre por su boca y por sus ojos. El intervalo de oscuridad se agrieta. Deja pasar una réplica.
> –Tenemos la culpa. Nosotros lo llamamos y El no vino. ¡Hum! ...esto es grave. ¿Se ha calculado cuántos hombres lo llaman a Dios en la noche? No importa que lo llamen para resolver sus asuntos personales. ¡Y cuántas almas están gritando despacio, despacito: ¡Dios, no me abandones, por favor!" ¿Se ha calculado cuántas criaturas antes de dormirse rezan a hurtadillas del padre oblicuo en la cama o de la madre detenida frente a un ropero entreabierto: "no nos dejes, Dios, por favor"? [NCC II 151]

Both this passage and the one we have quoted from the earlier novel are, of course, travesties of Christ's words on the cross. It is particularly important to understand at this stage of our enquiry that the negation of God is allied, here as elsewhere, to the godlessness of modern life. Erdosain is dismayed at the lack of response from God and his anguish is expressed through technical imagery. "Es como si le encarrilaran el pensamiento en una elíptica metálica." This image in its turn transmutes the anguish into urban terms so that technological growth of society has taken place "al margen de Dios". "Cada vez más existencias, más edificios, más dolor. Cárceles, hospitales, rascacielos, superrascacielos, subterráneos, minas, arsenales, turbinas, dínamos, socavones de tierra, rieles: más abajo vidas, suma de vidas. –Al margen de Dios se ha realizado todo esto. Y este Dios, decime, ¿qué hiciste por nosotros?" [NCC II 151]. We notice how deftly Arlt moves from existences and buildings to the concept of grief, all uttered in the same breath, for not only is God remote (and therefore *canalla*) but man is to blame ("tenemos la culpa") for his lunacy and obstinacy in creating social conditions in which God has ceased to have any meaning or existence. Throughout Arlt's writing, God is seen as man's creation, as an entity which might serve man's craving for a view of the stars. The obverse of this argument lies in man's ability to cut himself off from God and this, too, figures importantly in Arlt's thinking, drawing him once again near to Dostoevskian concepts. In *Los siete locos* Erdosain, like Raskolnikov, determines to instigate a crime –"the murder" of Barsut– as a means of affirming his own existence. What concerns us here are the religious and metaphysical assumptions to which this decision gives rise for, as may be seen, not only is God silent but man, too, is capable of promoting his own removal from God and therefore his anguished alienation from all created things. Erdosain recounts to Hipólita how the discovery of the idea of the elimination of Barsut has opened up new dimensions in his life, in that he now has it in his own hands to destroy his connections with God and mankind alike.

–Ahora he llegado al final. Mi vida es un horror... . Necesito crearme complicaciones ... y cometer el pecado. No me mire. Posiblemente ... vea ... el pecado no es una falta ... yo he llegado a darme cuenta de que el pecado es un acto por el cual el hombre rompe el débil hilo que lo mantenía unido a Dios. Dios lo está negado para siempre. Aunque la vida de ese hombre después del pecado se hiciera más pura que la del más puro santo, no podría llegar jamás hasta Dios [NCC I 347].

So it is that man's loss of God forms the bedrock of the Astrólogo's ideas on the great revolution rather than the hotch-potch of ideology culled, deliberately, from fascism, communism, theosophy and the like. "No sé si nuestra revolución será bolchevique o fascista," he asserts triumphantly. "A veces me inclino a creer que lo mejor que se puede hacer es preparar una ensalada rusa que ni Dios la entienda." [NCC I 182] It is towards man's *metaphysical* needs that the revolution is to be aimed. The Astrólogo's revolution is not one of bread nor even of liberty, but of new gods. Since man cannot live without a metaphysical lie, he perversely announces, "...Como en una farmacia, tendremos las mentiras perfectas y diversas, rotuladas para las enfermedades más fantásticas del entendimiento y del alma". Here we see Arlt's sombre humour poking through the anguish of the human condition. (Too little has been made of his black humour; too many ingenuous revolutionaries have been prepared to take him seriously about the revolution). Man will be re-born into the age of miracles, cries the Astrólogo; he will become "un millonario de fe". At night, the revolutionaries will project on to the clouds with enormous reflectors the entry of the just into Heaven. They themselves (the seven madmen) will become gods, handing down miracles and divine lies to the populace. (How well Arlt knew how to stand his own truths on their head!) "Si Dios no existe" suggests Ergueta, the religious maniac "hay que guardar el secreto. ¿Qué será de la tierra si los hombres supieran que Dios no existe?"

The aspirations of these characters are not always directed towards deistic absolutes and solutions. However, what is certain is that the impossibility of attaining their high-flown goals of purity, truth, self-affirmation and beauty is the motive force behind them all, barring only the bourgeois materialists against whom Arlt persistently hurls his invective. Nor would it be an exaggeration to see this same force at work in Arlt himself. It takes the form of a hypersensitive idealism which, failing to find reflection or satisfaction in surrounding society, is turned in on itself. Like Céline, writing during the same period, when confronted by society's failure to live up to these ideals he takes refuge in an apparently callous cynicism and a base view of life. Man is thus reduced to an animal –to a worm even– and his noblest functions are seen in a purely mechanistic light.

> ¡Cuántas cosas involuntarias sabe! Y la principal: que a lo largo de todos los caminos del mundo hay casitas, chatas o con techos en declive, o con tejados a dos aguas, con empalizadas, y que en estas casas el gusano humano nace, lanza pequeños gritos, es amamantado por un monstruo pálido y hediondo, crece, aprende un idioma que tantos otros millones de gusanos ignoran, y finalmente es oprimido por su prójimo o esclaviza a otros [NCC II 159].

As we shall see presently, this debased view of the world, whilst breaking new ground in Argentina, is typical of much writing that was taking place elsewhere during this period. As Dardo Cúneo puts it: "El asunto de su parte es seguir la pista de la realidad en sus desempeños más sórdidos, en sus travesuras más crueles, en sus inapelables desesperaciones (como si tratara de un cronista de la sección Policía, designado por Dios), o, por lo contrario – apuntar con todos los júbilos inocentes hacia las esperas de los hombres rumbo a la utopía. Término medio, ninguno. O se mueve en la roña. O se sobrevive en la redención. Es decir, la humillación o la bienaventuranza".[19]

Others have seen Arlt's destructive and negative attitudes in a different light. Marta Molinari felt that he was incapable of embracing beauty, love or goodness and that he came to suspect that everything was an empty shell. There remained nothing for him, she says, either in the human world or in the one beyond. But he was not so made that he could accept this state of affairs without anguish. "Siente la necesidad de seguir probando, de buscar si algo resiste en su contorno o en su entraña; y al mismo tiempo, la angustia de no encontrarlo lo empuja a insistir en el anonadamiento con atracción obsesiva, a asegurarse que todo es abyección, odiando al mundo porque lo ha engañado, porque no puede creer en él, y porque encuentra que él mismo no tiene razón de ser al estar obligado a vivir en ese mundo, sin otros mundos posibles."[20] If Molinari's argument is correct, it seems unlikely that Arlt's characters would be able to sustain their yearning for those very absolutes which, she contends, he himself was unable to accept. She is nearer the mark when she writes "sin otros mundos posibles". Arlt's driving force is an unachievable and sometimes misplaced idealism which is worked out, in the novels, either in fantasies or in disgust and nausea. If one turns to his *Aguafuertes porteñas*, with their warmth of understanding and acuteness of eye, it is clear that he came to terms with this ambivalent attitude, preserving a deep regard for struggling mankind, in its despair and petty folly.

Social origins of anguish

Arlt was the first novelist in Argentina to realize the deleterious effect that urban technological society was having (and would continue to have) on the individual's search for happiness and to forge his novels from this material, thus bringing the city into the novel as a central force. Others like Gálvez before him had dealt with urban themes (particularly prostitution, in *Nacha Regules*) but none of them had incorporated man's urban surroundings in so rotund a manner so that the city becomes the very protagonist of his work. As the Buscador de Oro says in *Los siete locos*, what the Astrólogo proposes with his wild-eyed schemes for revolution is "la salvación del alma de los hombres agotados por la mecanización de nuestra civilización" [NCC I 294]. "¿Sabe usted lo que es el proletariado. anarquista, socialista, de nuestras ciudades? Un rebaño de corbardes. En vez de irse a romper el alma a la montaña y a los campos, prefieren las comodidades y los divertimientos a la heroica soledad del desierto ... Las ciudades son los cánceres del mundo". As in Mallea's works where the city is seen as implacably hostile to indigenous dweller and immigrant alike, so too in Arlt the city is always more than a mere background to man's activities.[21] It absorbs and destroys him, intruding into his life, moulding it into patterns which are alien to his happiness and nobility. As Núñez says: "...la ciudad configura psicológicamente a los hombres, deformándolos, imponiéndoles una 'vida gris' que no pueden superar porque son demasiado débiles".[22] Of course, Arlt was far from being alone in this reaction to the dehumanizing forces of urban life; on an international level, the theme was already widespread. North American novelists of the pre-war era, like Upton Sinclair, admittedly more socialist in inspiration and proposal, were creating a comparable picture of the urban hell that man was building for himself, the significant difference being that whilst Sinclair attributes these conditions to a boss class, Arlt seems to regard them as inherent in man's urban existence. Sinclair's picture of Chicago, with its stockyards and canning factories in which the workers are almost more wretched than the beasts they are called upon to slaughter, is not dissimilar in its general burden to Arlt's phantasmagoric vision of Buenos Aires. It is useful to set the two writers side by side and compare Jurgis's experience of the inhospitality of Chicago (he was an immigrant, of course) at the turn of the century with that of Erdosain's reaction to Buenos Aires:

> He saw the world of civilization then more plainly than ever he had seen it before; a world in which nothing counted but brutal might, an order devised by those who possessed it for subjugation of those who did not. He was one of the latter; and all outdoors, all life, was to him one colossal prison, which he paced like a pent-up tiger, trying one bar after another, and finding them all beyond his power. He had lost in the fierce battle of greed, and so was doomed to be exterminated; and all society was busied to see that he did not escape the sentence. Everywhere that he turned were prison-bars, and hostile eyes following him; the well-fed sleek policemen, from whose glances he shrank, and who seemed to grip their clubs more tightly when they saw him; the saloon-keepers who never ceased to watch him whilst he was in their places, who were jealous of every moment he lingered after he had paid his money; the hurrying throngs upon the streets, who were deaf to his entreaties, oblivious of his very existence, and savage and contemptuous when he forced himself upon them. They had their own affairs, and there was no place for him amongst them.[23]

Here we have the same sense of despair and exclusion from society, the irreparable loneliness and the same attack on the possessive mentality of the owning classes against which Arlt inveighs so virulently. Sinclair was, of course, a social realist whilst Arlt takes these anguished feelings and translates them into something bordering on expressionistic fantasy more akin to Fritz Lang's view of the metropolis. According to Arlt, man is a plague spreading over the whole world. Wherever Erdosain might go to seek peace, there man will also be. "Adonde vayas encontrarás la peste hombre y la peste mujer" he cries [NCC II 175]. How prophetic to have realized by the year of 1930 what now seems likely to become to world's most intractable problem by the year 2000! Not only do the tentacles of man's civilization reach everywhere but it is a civilization which is destructive of man himself. "La sociedad, para el personaje argentino, es un engranaje insensible, ciego, que mata o mutila ... El terror de ser absorbido por esa fuerza ciega les devora el alma a todos".[24] Thus Arlt writes of Erdosain that "la terrible civilización lo había metido dentro de un chaleco de fuerza del que no se podía escapar" [NCC I 254].

> Pero él quiere escaparse de las prisiones de cemento, hierro y cristal, más cargadas que condensadores eléctricos. Los jazzbands chillan y serruchan el aire de ozono de las grandes ciudades. Son conciertos de monos humanos que se queman el trasero. Erdosain piensa con terror en las cocottes" que ganan cinco mil dólares semanales, y en los hombres que tienen atravesados los maxilares por dolores tetánicos. Erdosain quiere escaparse de la civilización; dormir en el sol de la noche, que gira siniestro y silencioso al final de un viaje cuyos boletos vende la muerte [NCC II 201].

It will be seen how the compenetration of human frustration and the babylonic structure of the metropolis are captured by Arlt in this almost expressionistic outburst of anguish and ultimate death-wish.

Arlt is a typical product of his age, if untypical of Argentina. His fiction is more akin to European and North American norms than to indigenous ones. It is most significant that his first novel was published in the same year as *Don Segundo Sombra*, the one representing the opening up of a whole new process in Argentine literature –the true urban novel– and the other, the impressive culmination of a great myth. Noë Jitrik points out that 1926 is a veritable watershed in Argentine writing –"un año de clarificación" he calls it– with the publication of Arlt's *El juguete rabioso*, Quiroga's *Los desterrados*, Larreta's *Zogoibi* and Güiraldes's *Don Segundo Sombra*, each of which opens up or closes a process.[25] (He fails to record that the same year saw the publication of Mallea's first work also.) It is in a way regrettable, but not surprising, that Argentine writing should have become known in Europe and the USA (at least, until the arrival of Borges as an international cult figure) for its *gaucho* myth, particularly through the many translations of Güiraldes's work, whilst concurrently there was developing a sturdy tradition of urban literature from the 1920s onwards. In this respect, Arlt was the first to share, with European writers of the twenties, in the widespread revulsion and disillusion born of the First World War, whence, in content alone, the presence of poisonous gases, phosgene plants, gassed soldiers and constant talk of annihilation by bombardment in *Los siete locos* and more so in *Los lanzallamas*. He had also read the classic anti-war books stemming from the early post-war years, particularly Barbusse. In one of his *Agufuertes* he refers to Barbusse and writers like him "...que provocan este maravilloso y terrible fenómeno de simpatía humana. Hacen que seres, hombres y mujeres, que viven bajo distintos climas, se comprendan en la distancia porque en el escritor se reconocen iguales; iguales en sus impulsos, en sus esperanzas, en sus ideales. Y hasta se llega a esta conclusión: un escritor que sea así, no tiene nada que ver con la literatura. Está fuera de la literatura. Pero, en cambio, está con los hombres, y eso es lo necesario; estar en alma, con todos, junto a todos" [AP 203].

It might be difficult to show that Arlt was influenced by Barbusse, other than in his general attitudes, as the above plea for committed literature would show, but it is striking to what extent the nausea to which he gives full vent finds expression in many pages that might well have been culled straight from Céline's *Voyage au bout de la nuit*. There is, as is now recognized, a straight line of descent from Dostoevsky through Céline to Sartre and the modern French existentialists. Arlt, in a way, establishes his own *existentialisme avant la lettre* in Buenos Aires at a much earlier date. There is no cross-connection between Arlt and Céline to the best of our knowledge but many passages from the former, with their nauseous reaction to city life, might readily be transplanted into Céline, or vice versa. One or two quotations will help to make this clear. Consider the bitter and rancorous outburst of Erdosain when confronted by bourgeois shopkeepers as he proceeds through Buenos Aires:

> Entonces su irritación se volvió contra la bestial felicidad de los tenderos, que a los puertas de sus covachas escupían a la oblicuidad de la lluvia. Se imaginó que estaban tramando eternos chanchullos, mientras que sus desventradas mujeres se dejaban ver desde las trastiendas, extendiendo manteles en las mesas cojas, arramblando ignobles guisotes que al ser descubiertos en la fuentes arrojaban a la calle flatulencias de pimentón y de sebo, y ásperos relentes de milanesas recalentadas [NCC I 305].

The tone of *asco* in this passage, brimming over into almost total revulsion, is wholly remininscent of the tone that Céline was striking in his descriptions of Paris and New York during the same period.[26] Compare Céline, in *Voyage au bout de la nuit*, published in 1932:

> Un seul dimanche à les voir se distraire, ça suffirait pour vous enlever à toujours le goût de la rigolade. Autour du métro, près des bastions croustille, endémique, l'odeur des guerres qui traînent, des relents de villages mi-brûlés, mal cuits, des révolutions qui avortent, des commerces en faillitte. Les chiffonniers de la zone brûlent depuis des saisons les mêmes petits tas humides dans les fossés à contre-vent. C'est des barbares à la manque ces biffins pleins de litrons et de fatigue. Ils vont tousser au Dispensaire d'à-côté, au lieu de balancer les tramways dans les glacis et d'aller pisser dans l'octroi un bon coup. Quand la guerre elle reviendra, la prochaine, ils feront encore une fois fortune à vendre de peaux de rats, de la cocaïne et des masques en tôle ondulée.[27]

Both are concerned, of course, to *épater le bourgeois*, but even where they are purely descriptive, their prose is invested with a revulsion which springs from their doom-ridden view of man as an urban animal. Their vision is based on a wide perspective in which man is reduced to an ant-like creature, struggling, frenzied, in a hostile city environment. Compare Céline's picture of frantic Ford workers with Arlt's description of factories and dwellings and foreign workers reduced to the same desperate activity as in his French counterpart's work:

> Et j'ai vu en effet des grands bâtiments trapus et vitrés, des sortes de cages à mouches sans fin, dans lesquelles on discernait des hommes à remuer, mais remuer à peine, comme s'ils ne se débattaient que faiblement contre je ne sais quoi d'impossible. C'était ça Ford? Et puis tout autour et au-dessus jusqu'au ciel un bruit lourd et multiple et sourd de torrent d'appareils, dur, l'entêtement des mécaniques à tourner, rouler, gémir, toujours prêts à casser et ne cassant jamais.[28]

Arlt's prose is more technical, more coloured but nonetheless effective:

> Luego el camino se bifurca y entran nuevamente en la zona de las barracas que desparraman hedores de sangre, lana y grasa; usinas de las que se escapan vaharadas de ácido sulfúrico y de azufre quemado; calles donde, entre muros rojos, zumba maravilloso un equipo de dínamos y transformadores humeando

aceite recalentado. Los hombres que descargan carbón y tienen el pelo rubio y rojo se calafatean en los bares ortodoxos y hablan un imposible idioma de Checoslovaquia, Grecia y los Balcanes [NCC II 139].

No doubt the psychological parallels between Arlt and Céline would also bear scrutiny, for it would seem that both share a frustrated idealism and fall back upon a case-hardened cynicism as a means of survival in a relentlessly adverse world. Their nausea is a safety valve used to relieve the pressure of their boiling indignation at the defective state of society. This is the first of the defence mechanisms within Arlt's reach and he makes full play with it. [29]

Psychological origins of anguish

All Arlt's major characters are stunted in one sense or another, bearing the mark of some tragedy, lack of fulfilment or psychological malformation which leads to their anguished condition. "¿Creía Arlt en lo que escribía?" asks Etchenique. "Es difícil suponer que cuando febrilmente aferrado a su máquina pasaba noches enteras desarmando el mundo interior que lo torturaba, tenía presente la realidad. Sumido en la pasión creadora, un escritor suele levantar la vista a observar a su alrededor. Arlt no la levantaba nunca. Su realidad es la de ese universo confuso y deshilvanado de donde saca y lanza a la vida una galería de personajes monstruosos y pueriles que en medio de la bruma, torpes y atolondrados, se mueven, tropiezan, dan manotazos, hablan". [30] The characters suffer from a distinct tendency towards caricature and the grotesque, more so as his fiction advances. While in *El juguete rabioso*, even the brief appearance of Monti, the irascible paper merchant who employs Silvio, or the briefer appearance of Dio Fetente, picaresque as they are, leaves the reader with an impression of having encountered a person existing in his own right, from *Los siete locos* onwards the characters are much more at the mercy of their creator, or at least of some warped aspect of the temperament with which he has endowed them, and they are manipulated like puppets. There can be no doubt that this is part of his design for his fiction. Thus the Astrólogo (perhaps representing Arlt the creator?) plays God to the rest of the characters in the small world in which he moves. One night, when he is alone, he hoists on to a cord the marionettes which epitomize the rest of the revolutionaries. He is only too aware of the truth that they are all victims of their own anguish, beginning with himself, the castrated hero, and that their destiny is inexorable, closing in on them slowly as the work advances, as they stumble from one paroxysm of despair to the next. To quote Etchenique again: "Los personajes de Arlt nunca se apresuran. Carecen del sentido de la proporción, de la medida del tiempo y de la pasión y están ligados entre sí por la desesperación." [31] Here she has her finger on a vital problem which she has failed to resolve. This is the very weakness of Arlt's characters. They are anguished beyond hope of redemption and therefore, in the literary sense, incapable of further development. Arlt failed to realize that whereas Dostoevsky's creations are also prey to their own passions and defects, they fall victim only after a titanic struggle. Erdosain, the Astrólogo, Hipólita, el Hombre que vio a la Partera, el Rufián Melancólico, Ergueta, are all prisoners in a plaster cast of Arlt's making, "...seres condenados a ser lo que son".[32] This follows unavoidably from the choice of anguish as their main motivating force. They live and die in anguish, for they are incapable of assuming different proportions as the work advances, constrained by definition from the start. The anguish which is in Erdosain at the beginning of *Los siete locos* is the very same force that drives him irrevocably to the murder of María la Bizca at the end of *Los lanzallamas* and to atone by taking his own life. The only characters who escape this predetermination are the peripheral ones, like la Bizca's mother, Doña Ignacia, who brings a welcome air of human folly with her petty snobbery and her insistence on her lineage, allowing her daughter (an over-developed fourteen year old) to have relations meanwhile with a married man of almost thirty, lineage notwithstanding. (Erdosain has caught the daughter "...en el zaguán con la mano en la bragueta de un hombre", where, as he affirms, "no ha ido a buscar rosas o jazmines".) Not that the characters are incapable of some unusual or senseless act; the incorporation of the *acte gratuit* sees to that. But in the final analysis, they are unable to surprise us simply because they are trapped within their own mould, much as Mallea's great isolates fail to jar the reader out of his complacent assumptions because their loneliness, too, is incapable of being transcended.[33]

Few of the characters in Arlt's novels enjoy a substantiated psychological background. Even in the case of those for whom some previous understanding *is* available, we are asked to scale some unlikely heights before we reach a clear view. The reader is confronted by a group of social and psychological deviants with little or no reason given to account for their condition, except for the general assumption of the omnipresence of anguish in contemporary society. We know that the Astrólogo fell over a banister rail and castrated himself (!); the Rufián Melancólico was once a teacher of mathematics but has turned his hand to more profitable ends by keeping three women for prostitution. An improbable but amusing tale is told to account for the condition of "El Hombre que vio a la Partera", a name which itself hints at the contents of his story. Ergueta has been too fundamental in his interpretation of certain passages from the Bible and forsaken his legitimate profession as a druggist in order to take a prostitute to wife, since the Bible says: "...y salvaré la coja y recogeré la descarriada". Even from this brief list, two things are apparent: the main characters are not only on the edge of lunacy, as Arlt's title would suggest, but they also inhabit a land of half-truths where the author expects his reader sometimes to take them seriously and sometimes not, with the possible exception of Erdosain, his wife Elsa and Hipólita. If we lose sight of his black humour, the carpet will be pulled from under our feet. Not for nothing is Arlt attracted to the idea of writing about madmen. Like Hamlet using the players, he allows himself the privilege of revealing certain truths without the need for final substantiation. The case is different with Erdosain, for he is the one character in whom we are consistently asked to believe, madman or not, since it is apparent that he carries too much of Arlt himself for it to be otherwise.[34] He is therefore the one character whose anguish called for a substantial psychological elucidation.

The first incident in *Los siete locos* presents us with the immediate circumstances of his life. He has been a debt-collector for a sugar company, misappropriated certain funds, has been given hours in which to make restitution and, in the meantime, is dismissed. Obviously, this background is nothing more than a convenient hook on which to hang the story, for immediately thereafter the reader is plunged into a harrowing exposition of his grave state of anguish which is, after all, connected to the theft in a tangential way only. If anything, the theft is rather a product of his state of anguish. Here, it becomes more difficult to maintain the distinction that we have drawn between the concepts of anguish and humiliation, for, with Erdosain, they now become one. Arlt makes quite clear that he does not intend the protagonist's social circumstances to be seen as the only key to his inner condition, since the latter antedates the former in a quite explicit way. "Sabía que era un ladrón. Pero la categoría en que se colocaba no le interesaba. Quizás la palabra ladrón no estuviera en consonancia con su estado interior. Existía otro sentimiento y ése era el silencio circular entrado como un cilindro de acero en la masa de su cráneo, de tal modo que lo dejaba sordo para todo aquello que no se relacionara con su desdicha" [NCC I 161]. As we saw in an earlier reference, Erdosain had gone so far as to believe that anguish "flotaba en el aire". So here, at the very beginning of his story, it is apparent that he suffers simply because all mankind suffers. He believes in the existence of "una zona de angustia" which floats at a height of two metres above the level of the city. "Esta zona de angustia era la consecuencia del sufrimiento de los hombres. Y como una nube de gas venenoso se trasladaba pesadamente de un punto a otro, penetrando murallas y atravesando los edificios, sin perder su forma plana y horizontal; angustia de dos dimensiones que guillotinando las gargantas dejaba en estas un regusto de sollozo" [NCC I 161]. The manner in which this suffering is interlaced with Erdosain's desire for humiliation and with his fantasies is important to our considerations. Once his condition has been posited, it is significant that the movement of his mind is, firstly, towards the fabrication of a fantasy and, secondly, towards the realization that suffering is a necessity in his existence, in that he longs for it and seeks to humiliate himself through it.

En esas circunstancias compaginaba insensateces. Llegó a imaginarse que los ricos, aburridos de escuchar las quejas de los miserables, construyeron jaulones tremendos que arrastraban cuadrillas de caballos. Verdugos escogidos por su fortaleza cazaban a los tristes con lazo de acogotar perros, llegándole a ser visible cierta escena: una madre, alta y desmelenada, corría tras el jaulón de donde, entre los barrotes, la llamaba su hijo tuerto, hasta que un "perrero", aburrido de oírla gritar, la desmayó a fuerza de golpes en la cabeza, con el mango del lazo [NCC I 162].

Not only does this grotesque fantasy contain the seeds of many such imaginings which are to follow in these novels (with their fixation on imprisonment in cages, the concept of one-eyedness and gratuitous violence), it also represents the first withdrawal from or palliation of anguish attempted by Erdosain. Ensuing upon this fantasy sequence, there erupts the sense of self-abasement which will also become characteristic. "–Pero ¿qué alma, qué alma es la que tengo yo?– y como su imaginación conservaba el impulso motor que le había impreso la pesadilla, continuaba–: yo debo haber nacido para lacayo, uno de esos lacayos perfumados y viles con quienes las prostitutas ricas se hacen prender los broches del portasenos, mientras el amante fuma un cigarro recostado en el sofa". In the jargon of "el impulso motor" we have a clue to the quasi-scientific inspiration of Arlt's interest in sexual and psychological deviation, for it is important to remember that he was writing in the late twenties when psychoanalysis was beginning to make great strides. "Sí, yo soy un lacayo. Tengo el alma de un verdadero lacayo – y apretaba los dientes de satisfacción al insultarse y rebajarse de ese modo ante sí mismo" [NCC I 163]. Not only are we faced by gratuitous pornographic details, common enough in these novels, but Arlt is determined to plunge his reader as quickly as possible into the devil/saint dichotomy that he sees as inherent in man's condition and to confront him brusquely with his concept of saintliness through humiliation and self-immolation. This idea was to remain a constant in his fictional works, as may be seen from the fact that the Astrólogo underlines to Hipólita in *Los lanzallamas* that "Cuando un hombre lleva el demonio en el cuerpo, busca a Dios mediante pecados terribles, así su remordimiento será más intenso y espantoso". So it is that Erdosain, in his despair, goes out in search of card-playing and prostitutes, "...quizá buscando en el naipe y en la hembra una consolación brutal y triste, quizá *buscando en todo lo más vil y humilde cierta certidumbre de pureza que lo salvara definitivamente*" [NCC I 166. (My italics)]. Thereafter, anguish and self-abasement go hand in hand throughout the two major novels, a product of Erdosain's fruitless search for purity and happiness. It is sometimes impossible to distinguish whether Arlt himself observes any difference, for the two terms are often used indiscriminately.

As the novels progress, however, apart from his conviction of the omnipresence of suffering in human life, Arlt sees fit to reveal certain specific reasons for his protagonist's febrile condition. These may be classified broadly into sexual and childhood experiences, as one might expect, since the possibilities of Freudian psychology were now dawning upon him. Typically, his views on sex are characterized by an ambivalent approach, as will become clear when we analyse this aspect of his writing. All three mature novels are peppered with sexual scenes, references to masturbation and to the sexual habits of the middle class, from which, of course, his characters proceed. Behind these references, there is no attempt at titillation but rather an all-pervading sense of guilt, as though bodily contact (or more specifically genital contact) sapped the aspiration towards purity which drives the characters along. Thus it is Erdosain's sexual relationship with la Bizca, desiring her on the one hand and wishing to punish her on the other, that impels him to murder her, when she tries to draw him on to her in the middle of the night. There is a basic puritanism in all these characters' sexual lives: "...Esa severidad religiosa con la que el sexo es visto en las novelas de Arlt" Masotta calls it.[35] In line with Arlt's ironic humour, the only two persons to achieve a satisfactory relationship are Hipólita and El Astrólogo, presumably *because* the latter is castrated and not in spite of it! In fact, on discovering his castration, Hipólita, who has worked her way through a hard apprenticeship in prostitution, is enraptured. "–Como ¿vos también? ... un gran dolor ... Entonces somos iguales ... Yo tampoco he sentido nada, nunca, junto a ningún hombre ... y sos ... el único hombre. ¡Qué vida!" [NCC II 23]. It is coincidental, presumably, that at the end of the two novels the only two characters who are spared a fate of retribution are these two "lovers", who are never seen again.

Erdosain had always believed that a man married "para estar siempre junto a su mujer y gozar la alegría de verse a todas horas". He never kissed his wife "porque además creía que 'a una señorita no debe besársela' ". She was the true expression of purity, perfection and candour and, therefore, when she undresses on their wedding-night, he feels he must turn away, blushing to the roots of his hair. He then gets into bed with his trousers on, – always the same proclivity towards black humour in Arlt, teetering on the edge of tragedy! "¿No tenés miedo de que se te arruguen?" she asks. "¡Sacátelos, zoncito!" But the damage is already latent in Erdosain. "Más tarde, una distancia misteriosa la separó a Elsa de Erdosain. Se entregaba a él, pero con repugnancia, defraudada quién sabe en qué" [NCC I 243]. After a violent scene in which their frustration and rancour plumb the depths of agony, Arlt writes simply: "Y apareció en él la

angustia", inviting us to believe that therein lies the whole problem.
However, in *Los lanzallamas*, Elsa, now abandoned by her lover and
seeking refuge in a convent, recounts her story to the Mother Superior.
From this harrowing account, we learn that Erdosain's complicated desire
for humiliation and his insistence on introducing a prostitute into the
marital household, with whom he has maintained the purest of relations,
of course, have also contributed in no small measure to the breakdown of
their marriage. Following a "flashback" to the nuptial scene, there are
long sequences in which her husband's carnal necessities are explored, not
in a uniquely sexual sense, although it is finally by sexual means that his
anguish is assuaged. The only antidote to his failed endeavours lies in "el
delicioso terror de la masturbación".

The childhood origins of Erdosain's anguish are likewise divided between the two novels, one chapter in each, having to do with his relations
with his father. Just as with Mallea's isolates, no mention is made of the
mother and one is left to assume that the boy was brought up without
maternal care. (This is contrary to what occurs in his first novel where no
mention is made of the father and the mother looms large as a dominant
figure in the adolescent Silvio's life.) But Mallea makes the psychological
background quite specific in all cases; Arlt is deliberately vague. However,
Arlt's Erdosain shares with Mallea's characters the same cruel and harsh
father. Some critics have made great play with the episodes in which
Erdosain recounts how his father would beat him and humiliate him as a
child. Maldavsky in particular goes to great lengths to impose a Freudian
interpretation on the description of the building and subsequent destruction of the child's sandcastle and of the visit of the gassed soldier to
Erdosain. He ties in the gassing of the man with Arlt's (supposed) lack of
grief at the death of his father, not to mention his bronchial pneumonia at
the age of twenty. This is difficult enough to swallow, but the gloss he
puts on the simple incident in which the child goes into the hen-run,
builds a sandcastle and then destroys it by pelting it with stones seems to
be a triumph of psychological theory over common sense.[36] In our opinion,
such interpretations align the man and his work somewhat too strictly.
One would not wish to gainsay that such parallels exist. It is a well
substantiated fact that Arlt's father was extremely severe. According to
his mother, the father once refused to speak to the boy for three *years*!
Larra writes as follows: "La misma madre ha certificado las diferencias
entre el novelista y su padre. 'Nadie supo nunca lo que Roberto ha
sufrido; tres años estuvo sin hablarle. Su primera juventud fue muy trágica,
su vida y la mía fue una tragedia, por esto sus escritos tienen mucha
angustia' ".[37] And in the much-quoted and infamous scene in *Los siete
locos* where Erdosain allows his wife to be abducted by her lover under
his very nose, almost conniving at this ultimate degradation, his protagonist

declares: "Quien comenzó este feroz trabajo de humillación fue mi padre. Cuando yo tenía diez años y había cometido alguna falta, me decía: 'Mañana te pegaré' " [NCC I 204]. And this, effectively, is what the father does, to such a degree that the child develops a gross inferiority complex: "y esa sensación de que el alma se esondía avergonzada dentro de mi misma carne, me aniquilaba todo coraje". He would drag him from his childhood games to make him scrub the floor, calling him "perro" and "imbécil" the while. "El chiquillo no podía menos de comparar su vida con la de otros compañeros. Esos niños tenían padres que los venían a buscar a la salida de la escuela. A él su padre no lo besaba nunca. ¿Por qué? En cambio, lo humillaba continuamente" [NCC II 164]. Whilst not wishing to doubt the veracity of these experiences, whether in Arlt himself or as reflected in his characters, they nevertheless form an excrescence on the novel in the artistic sense. However, it is imperative to see them in the light of the contemporary interest in psychology and the growing vogue for psychoanalysis. Dostoevsky, who was convinced of the naturalness of the perverse whims and irrational conduct of mankind, saw no need to account for it.[38] This was to be left to the Freudians. Arlt was caught up, like so many writers in the 1920s, by the new science. Unfortunately, it does his characters little good as literary figures.

HUMILIATION AND THE SEARCH FOR SUFFERING

In Arlt, as in Dostoevsky, humiliation and the search for self-abasement are an atonement that the characters make for their pervading sense of guilt or, at least, a psychological state into which they force themselves in order to assuage their guilt complex. Apart from the proposed murder of Barsut in *Los siete locos*, which is aborted into black farce by the Astrólogo, Erdosain suffers from a deep-rooted remorse for a crime which is never made explicit: "El crimen que no se puede nombrar". It is left to the Rufián Melancólico, with his sharp awareness of human degradation, to scrutinize this aspect of the protagonist's temperament. He accuses Erdosain of having perpetrated some unspeakable crime, connecting it forcefully with his feelings of anguish. "No le pido que me cuente nada", he says to him. "Eso es asunto suyo. Pero yo he puesto el dedo en la llaga. Aunque usted diga que no con la boca, usted sabe en su interior que yo tengo razón. ... Sólo así se explicaría esa 'ansia de humillación' que hay en usted" [NCC II 45]. He pursues this enquiry, delving deeper into Erdosain's mentality, whilst the latter puts up the weakest of resistance. The link between this desire for humiliation and the phenomenon of alienation from one's fellow-men is made immediately explicit. "Esa 'ansia de humillación' que hay en usted es la siguiente sensación: Usted ha comprendido que no tiene derecho a acercarse a nadie, por el horrible crimen que cometió" [NCC II 46]. Thus the relationship between remorse and guilt, alienation and humiliation is a basic premise of Arlt's narrative. It is our belief that not only did Arlt discover the pattern for the expression of anguish in Dostoevsky, as he came upon the framework for his political arguments in *The Devils*,[2] but that he also followed the Russian into the labyrinthine concept of humiliation and degradation and the idea of saintliness through suffering. We hope to make these influences and affinities apparent as we proceed. However, it must be added at this juncture that what we shall demonstrate in no way detracts from Arlt's originality as a writer and commentator on *porteño* life. Had Arlt himself been a less anguished individual, it is unlikely that he would have chosen such themes for exploration, nor would he have approached them so successfully. It does not follow that his authenticity is impaired because of some outside influence, as a number of Argentine critics would seem to believe, thereby denying that such influences exist. As is well known, Dostoevsky admitted the great influence upon him of Gogol's exploitation of dreams and his analysis of demented individuals. He is none the less great for that.

As Gide and others have pointed out, there is a naturalness in Dostoevsky's exploration of humiliation when seen against the teachings of the Russian Orthodox Church, with its emphasis on this concept derived from the New Testament.[3] Gide observes that the idea of personal honour and pride has traditionally been quite different in Russia from that held in Western Europe, the former being much closer to the Gospels. "The notion of confession, not murmured low into priestly ears, but made openly, before any and all, comes up again and again almost with the quality of an obsession, in Dostoevsky's novels. When Raskolnikov has confessed his crime to Sonia, in *Crime and Punishment*, she advises him, as the one means of unburdening his soul, at once to prostrate himself in the public street and cry aloud, "I have the blood of a fellow-being on my hands'."[4] It is also vitally important to observe the distinction between humility and humiliation for, as Gide says, humility implies a measure of submission of the free will, whilst humiliation degrades and warps the soul. "It irritates, impoverishes and blights, inflicting a mortal hurt ill to heal." It is this kind of humiliation which is common in Arlt's characters who, by a process of innurement, come to yearn for the abject joys of their own abasement. Thus he writes in a footnote to the account of Erdosain's childhood: "En estos sucesos podríamos encontrar las raíces subconscientes de ese deseo de Erdosain hombre de contraer matrimonio con una mujer que le impusiera tareas humillantísimas para su dignidad" [NCC II 164]. To quote Gide again, in a most apposite statement: "It happens that some ... whose natures have been profoundly warped by humiliation, find as it were delight and satisfaction in the resultant degradation, loathsome though it be."

Before we make firm textual comparisons with Dostoevsky, let us examine how Arlt's characters take this concept for their own. We have already seen how their anguish is the product of an unfulfilled drive towards purity – "su incontrolable desenfrenado deseo de pureza" as Etchenique calls it. With humiliation, this becomes doubly obvious, as they strive to achieve saintliness through even greater abasement. Already in *El juguete rabioso* this sense of humiliation is present in embryonic shape. When the adolescent Silvio is obliged by his employer's wife to hump a great basket of chattels through the central streets of the city, following yet another row with her husband, he is made abjectly aware of his position as underdog. "Yo no detenía los ojos en nadie" he confesses, "tan humillado me sentía...". He delivers books to a young woman in her flat –a "cocotte" as Arlt insists– and the kiss that she plants flirtatiously on his lips arouses the wildest dreams and urges in the young boy. "...por el júbilo de poseerla y amarla haría las cosas más ignominiosas y las más dulces" he cries. (How intimately "lo ignominioso" and "lo dulce" go hand in hand, even at this stage!) One night he is ordered by Doña María to swab out the latrine, which is impossibly filthy. "Y obedecí sin decir palabra. Creo que yo buscaba motivos para multiplicar en mi interior una finalidad oscura", he adds. Her husband, too, humiliates him, searching him to ensure that he is not stealing books from his store. Silvio's reaction is one of submission, like that of an embryonic Erdosain: "No pude indignarme ni sonreír. Era necesario eso, sí, creo; era necesario que mi vida, la vida que durante nueve meses había nutrido con pena un vientre de mujer, sufriera todos los ultrajes, todas las humillaciones, todas las angustias" [NCC I 91]. He is made to wipe the floor, and, from this humble position, he is forced to ask delightful young women to remove their feet. He is sent out to do the shopping with an enormous basket; all manner of humiliation is heaped upon him and he accepts it willingly. "Posiblemente si me hubieran escupido a la cara, me limpiara tranquilo con el revés de la mano."

As yet, Arlt had not forged these feelings into the nauseating sense of submission that would oblige Erdosain to seek out the vilest possible brothels in order to abase himself, only to run out on a prostitute, leaving his money on the table, nor, as yet, into the saint-like search for degradation which manifests itself at the beginning of *Los siete locos*: "Porque a instantes su afán era de humillación, como él de los santos que besaban las llagas de los inmundos; no por compasión, sino para ser más indignos de la piedad de Dios, que se sentirá asqueado de verles buscar el cielo con pruebas tan repugnantes" [NCC I 163]. Erdosain is abandoned by his wife in favour of her lover, el Capitán, but it is not his grief that comes to the fore so much as his need to inflict greater suffering upon himself, as he consciously imagines the two of them in sexual relations. "Más fuerte que su miedo fue su necesidad de más terror, de más sufrimiento..." In a later "flashback", when he and Elsa are reviewing their sexual difficulties, her words of rejection inflict suffering on him. It is an experience that he nevertheless craves, masochistically: "Quería sufrir más aún, agotarse de dolor, desangrarse en un lento chorrear de angustia" [NCC I 240]. Later, in *Los lanzallamas*, Erdosain acutely analyses his own condition to the Rufián who, degraded as he is himself, recoils in horror and disgust at the depths to which Erdosain would sink. "Mi problema consiste en hundirme. En hundirme dentro de un chiquero. ¿Por qué? No sé. Pero me atrae la suciedad. Créalo. Quisiera vivir una existencia sórdida, sucia, hasta decir basta. Me gustaría 'hacer' el novio ... no me interrumpa. Hacer el novio en alguna casa católica, llena de muchachas. Casarme con una de ellas, la más despótica; ser un cornudo, y que esa familia asquerosa me obligara a trabajar, largándome a la calle con los indispensables veinte centavos para el tranvía" [NCC II 44]. This sequence, too long to quote in full, reveals Erdosain at his most introspective and self-analytical. He is clearly a classic case –although Arlt himself may never have realised it– of masochism verging on madness. Erich Fromm points out how masochism (and sadism, of course) is an attempt to transcend overwhelming feelings of separation and loneliness, in order to achieve a symbiotic union with another.[5] Both these perversions find ample expression in Arlt's works, on the one hand, in abject degradation and the search for suffering at the hands of another and, on the other hand, in the desire to inflict suffering revealed in the frequent gratuitous acts scattered throughout his narrative. Fromm maintains that the experience of separateness not only arouses anxiety but is the source of *all* anxiety. If this is so, humiliations suffered or inflicted must be seen as an attempt to secure others to our own existence, to bind them to us in the most agonizing of shared experiences. It is, of course, at the root of the love/hate relationships which so impressed Gide in Dostoevsky. So we find that not only does Erdosain yearn for suffering for himself but he seeks to humiliate his wife also. "Necesito tormentarte" he tells her. (The "necesito" should not escape us.) "Cuando estoy a tu lado me es indiferente verte sufrir; cuando te tengo lejos padezco una angustia enorme". "Pero hubiera querido verte sufrir más, verte humillada ante mí, arrancarte un grito ... ese grito que nunca has lanzado ... Decime ... ¿no será ése el secreto de mi conducta?" [NCC II 130 and 131].

    In the light of the foregoing ideas, not only the repugnant infliction of suffering but Erdosain's loathesome wallowing in his own degradation become more accessible. He adroitly translates his grief at his sexual failure in marriage into a search for self-abasement in the following passage: "Vos has deshecho mi vida. Ahora sé por qué no te me entregabas. ¡y me has obligado a masturbarme! ¡sí, a eso! Me has hecho un trapo de hombre. Debía matarte. El primero que venga podrá escupirme en la cara" [NCC I 241]. When Elsa finally recounts their relationship to the Mother Superior, she is convinced that her husband's search for suffering is at the bottom of their inability to succeed in marriage. "Buscaba ya el sufrimiento", she explains. Nor is Erdosain the only one to experience this urge towards humiliation and self-immolation. His cousin Barsut who has always held Elsa in high esteem but has consistently been rebuffed by her, also feels the need to humiliate her in his turn. Indeed, this was the motive that prompted his act of betrayal, for it was he who informed on Erdosain to his employers. And why? Simply to degrade his wife. "¿Te das cuenta? Yo te denuncié. Quería hacerte meter preso, quedarme con Elsa, humillarla [NCC I 215]. As Gide says, quoting the case of Lebedyev in *The Idiot*, who tortures General Ivolgin: "Here is one of the laws we can establish: the man who has suffered humiliation seeks to inflict humiliation in his turn. "Si te denuncié fue por eso", claims Barsut, "para humillarla a ella que siempre fue tan orgullosa conmigo". In a similar way, Barsut wishes to humiliate a young girl whom he had wished to marry but discovered she had slept with another man. His desire to become a great filmstar is based on this urge alone. "Quiero humillarla profundamente. No descansaré hasta alcanzar el máximum de altura. Es necesario que esa perra se encuentre con mi nombre en la ochava de cada esquina" [NCC II 225].

If, as we have said, self-abasement is induced by an all-pervading sense of guilt, it certainly falls more naturally into Dostoevsky's novels than it does in Arlt's, provided that we accept the thesis that it is consubstantial with Russian Orthodox teaching. In Arlt, one has the feeling that it is introduced in an intrusive and arbitrary manner at the beginning of *Los siete locos*, almost taking the reader by surprise. What is he to make of the following, from Erdosain the debt-collector, recently turned thief, a mere four pages into the novel?

> Sabía, ¡ah, qué bien lo sabía! que estaba gratuitamente ofendiendo, ensuciando su alma. Y el terror que experimenta el hombre que en una pesadilla cae al abismo en que no morirá, padecíalo él, mientras deliberadamente se iba enlodando [NCC I 163].

The concept is thrust suddenly into the work, as though Arlt had determined to incorporate it from the outset to startle the reader.

Turning now to Dostoevsky, it is obvious that the latter's all-out attack on the fallibility of reason and utopian thinking was calculated to appeal to the generation of Argentine intellectuals and writers of which Arlt forms a part, during the final rout of positivism. For example, Mallea's admiration for Berdyaev and the Russian thinker's inspiration in Dostoevsky must presumably account for his [Mallea's] dictum about "la inteligencia del corazón", so close to the stated belief of Dostoevsky that all great ideas come from the heart and not the head. The latter's attack on systematic and positivistic reasoning in *Notes from Underground* (1864) might well have provided a battle-hymn for the anti-positivist thinkers in Argentina. As he says, man is capable of going insane, on purpose, just to be immune from reason.[6] Of course, he does not stop there, for *Notes from Underground* carries the seeds of all his future great ideas, which he was to elaborate in his subsequent works: *Crime and Punishment* (1866), *The Idiot* (1868), *The Devils* (1871), *The Brothers Karamazov* (1879) –with which Arlt and his *porteño* contemporaries became familiar in the early 1920s– based on his hope of man's salvation through suffering and humiliation.

> I derived pleasure precisely from the blinding realization of my degradation; because I felt I was already up against the wall; that it was horrible but couldn't

be otherwise: that there was no way out and it was no longer possible to make myself into a different person.[7]

Cannot reason be wrong about what may be good for man, what might be advantageous to man? asks Dostoevsky. "Why cannot man like other things than his wellbeing? Maybe he likes suffering just as much. Maybe suffering is just as much to his advantage as wellbeing. In fact, man adores suffering. Passionately."[8] It is not necessary to labour the case for Dostoevsky's influence at this stage; in spite of numerous objections from Arlt's compatriots, which we shall examine briefly in due course, there can be little remaining doubt of the close inspiration that the Russian provides. But there are two concepts in Dostoevsky which require some detailed elaboration if we are to understand Arlt's thinking and its genesis: the exploitation of crime as a means to self-inquiry and self-affirmation and the use of the gratuitous act inflicted wilfully on others. Let us look at the latter first.

We have seen that Fromm considers the sadistic act to be an attempt to attach ourselves to another person, to escape from our own sense of isolation. The *acte gratuit*, which so impressed Gide in Dostoevsky's novels, is a manifestation of the same urge often, but not invariably, invested with sadistic cruelty. Arlt took the stratagem to great lengths, particularly in the relationships between his male and female characters. One incident will suffice to highlight the parallels and influences in this respect. In the delicate story "Ester Primavera", the unnamed narrator meets and apparently falls in love with Ester. He then perversely conceives the notion of gratuitously shattering this burgeoning relationship by telling her a lie, to the effect that he is married when he is not. The girl is overwhelmed. To compound the injury, he dispatches a calumnious letter in such a way that her family will receive it, heaping infamy upon the lie. The motivation behind this apparently senseless act is that she will be bound to him forever. "Que ella me tuviera tal aborrecimiento que en el futuro, aunque me arrodillara a su paso, fuera inútil en mí toda humillación. Yo sería el único hombre a quien odiaría con paciencia de eternidad" [NCC III 257]. It will readily be seen that this act closely reflects the central act in *Notes from Underground*, where the narrator consciously wounds Liza, the prostitute. Having slowly forged a relationship with her and allowed her to believe that he had come to "save" her (this, too, occurs elsewhere with a prostitute in Arlt) he coarsely hurls the truth at her. Like Ester, the girl is heartbroken. He is later gnawed by remorse, as in Arlt's character, but both remain steadfast in their contrariness. "And isn't it much better, I mused later, back at home, trying to soothe the living pain with my fantasies, for her to bear this humiliation as long as she lives, because humiliation is purification, because it causes the most corrosive, the most painful awareness? I'd have soiled her soul and tired her heart no later than tomorrow, but this insult and humiliation will never be extinguished in her...".[9] When one considers textual similarities, the case becomes even stronger. After the infamous incident, Arlt's protagonist comes across Ester in the street. "Ah", he says, "qué feliz sería si me diera una bofetada". "But I believe there have been moments when I'd have liked my face slapped" says Dostoevsky's character. "I say that in all seriousness – I'd have derived pleasure from this too".

Instances of mindless violence abound in Arlt's writing, sometimes as pieces of nonsense, as when Ergueta decides to urinate on a passer-by and invites the Basque Delavene to do the same. He does so, but the victim draws a revolver and shoots him on the spot. Delavene dies in great agony, as does the narrator in "Ester Primavera"; in the latter case, a lingering death by tuberculosis. Just as the insult against Ester lives on in the narrator's life, so, too, the Delavene incident remains in Ergieta's memory to haunt him forever. "...cuando Ergueta estaba borracho y se nombraba a Delavene, aquél se arrodillaba y con la lengua hacía una cruz en el polvo" [NCC I 316]. (Could there be a more grotesque, more Dostoevskian atonement?) Sometimes, the desire in Arlt's characters to degrade others by senseless and gratuitous violence is carried to loathesome lengths. On one occasion, Erdosian filthies a young woman's face in the mud in an excess of unmotivated spleen. He had associated with her *because* she was ugly, wishing to discover "hasta qué punto llegaba o podía llegar el dominio de una criatura inferior sobre un hombre superior" [NCC II 116]. On another, he recounts to Hipólita a gruesome story of how he once took delight in revealing to a little girl of nine "el misterio sexual, incitándola a que se dedicara a corromper a sus amiguitas..." [NCC I 347]. Even as early as *El juguete rabioso* senseless violence has a major part to play. As a young writer, Arlt was uncannily aware of the workings of the warped mind, at a time when urban delinquency had not reached anything like its present proportions. Thus, in one incident, Silvio casts a lighted match on to a wretched human form huddled in a doorway. When this mentality is turned against a person with whom the character enjoys an intimate relationship, as happens at the end of *El juguete*, we have a wholly Dostoevskian situation. Silvio and El Rengo have planned a robbery against an engineer's house. On the day of the assault, Silvio conceives the hideous notion of informing on his confederate. The motive behind this proposed betrayal is far from being an economic one; there is no question of personal gain, as is demonstrated by his ultimate refusal of a reward. It is, in fact, twofold: each part carries us forward into Arlt's later work. Firstly, the act of betrayal will permit Silvio to delve into his own conscience and discover hidden depths: "La angustia abrirá a mis ojos grandes horizontes espirituales" he says. "Yo no soy un perverso, soy un curioso de esta fuerza enorme que está en mí". Secondly, as with Ester Primavera (or Dostoevsky's prostitute), his victim will be bound to him forever. "Aunque pasen mil años[10] no podré olvidarme de la cara del Rengo. ¿Qué será de él? Dios lo sabe; pero el recuerdo del Rengo estará siempre en mi vida, será en mi espíritu como el recuerdo de un niño que se ha perdido. El podrá venir a escupirme en la cara y yo no le diré nada" [NCC I 154].

The first of these motives, the need to discover one's internal forces, leads us naturally into a consideration of crime as an antidote to suffering. Not now the spontaneous *acte gratuit*, but something monstrous and wholly premeditated that will reveal the person to himself and allow him to become something in life. "Ser a través del crimen" as Arlt calls it in one of his chapter-headings. To quote Fromm once again: "The basic need to fuse with another person so as to transcend the prison of one's separateness is closely related to another specifically human desire, that to know the 'secret of man' ". So Erdosain says, as the proposed murder approaches: "No estoy loco, ya que sé pensar, razonar. Me sube la curiosidad del asesinato...". The same theme finds its echo in Gide's *Les Caves du Vatican* when Lafcadio pushes his companion from the train. "Ce n'est pas tant des événements que j'ai curiosité, que de moi-même". With Arlt, it assumes major proportions and is allied to the general concept of evil as man's ultimate gesture of independence and self-assurance and of his deliberate remoteness from God. "...sólo el crimen puede afirmar mi existencia" cries Erdosain, "como sólo el mal afirma la presencia del hombre sobre la tierra" [NCC I 223]. After the incident in which he discovers his betrayal to his employers at the hands of Barsut, he determines that the latter must be annihilated. Like Raskolnikov, who is also haunted by his feelings of "utter despair and desolation", he concludes that he must perpetrate some act that will mobilize his will. As Raskolnikov puts it: "He had to make up his mind at all costs, do something, anything, – or renounce life altogether". The conclusion that both arrive at involves a gratuitous murder, that of the old woman money-lender with the Russian, the murder of Barsut with Arlt. Both proceed with their plan in order to investigate the forces latent within them. It is seen as an experiment, a gesture of self-affirmation. "Es necesario hacer algo. Clavar un suceso en medio de la civilización, que sea como una torre de acero" [NCC II 54]. The fact that the killing of Barsut is turned into a black farce by the Astrólogo, from which the intended victim is allowed to escape unscathed, belongs to Arlt's view of the double reality of life. Significantly, the aborting of the murder is not revealed to Erdosain, who continues to believe that Barsut is dead. In this way, the one great step in which he has had faith, which might have affirmed his existence in his own eyes, is snatched away from him. The only path left open to him is self-destruction.

It is useful to pause at this stage, and consider the attitudes of certain Argentine critics towards Dostoevsky's influence upon Arlt. Some have been chauvinistic, denying any such influence and exalting the national spirit of Arlt's work. Others, perhaps with a feeling of compromise, have called him "un dostoyevskiano".[11] Some have made quite positive assertions of affinities and influence. Regrettably, it has not been the practice of Arlt's compatriots to set the two side by side to consider the matter with evidence to hand. Writing about the genesis of *El juguete rabioso*, Jitrik invokes Arlt's juvenile reading of "folletines" and of Dostoevsky: "Arlt no tiene limitaciones en los recursos que emplea; sabe de Rocambole y lo mete, sabe de Dostoyevsky y lo pone, sabe de la imaginería de la aventura y no se retacea a que todos esos libros de fiebre y ensueño le brindan". There is no doubt that the first part, in particular, of *El juguete* suffers from echoes of his juvenile reading. In fact, Arlt makes this quite explicit, with his tongue in his cheek. "Entonces, yo soñaba con ser bandido y estrangular corregidores libidinosos; enderezaría entuertos, protegería a las viudas y me amarían singulares doncellas" [NCC I 37]. This puerile aspect of his writing stretches, in fact, far into his adult composition. In contrast to Jitrik, Larra maintains that too much emphasis had been placed on the supposed influence of Dostoevsky, that Arlt takes his creatures directly from the "carácter multiforme y babélico de Buenos Aires", that he himself had personally known all those whom he depicts in his novels.[12] These two considerations are not necessarily at variance, of course. We must recognize that Larra's study has strong left-wing overtones. As we noted in our introduction, it was he who suggested that the correct attitude towards Arlt was to accept his spirit of social criticism but to reject his tone of despair. This is to overlook the one quality that separates him from his precursors and many of his contemporaries. Argentine literature had never been lacking in social criticism; one has only to think of Gálvez's work, or even that of Payró or Fray Mocho, and the long tradition going back to Martel. Arlt feeds on this tradition but gives to it the existential dimension which was to become the keynote of a large part of Argentine writing during the following four decades.

A more redoubtable objection is that of Murena, not this time based on political considerations. Murena is the first to appreciate the existential argument. He readily acknowledges the affinity between Arlt and Dostoevsky, but denies the influence. He refers to Arlt's "ansias de ser" which drove him to grasp at the one quality in life which is particular to each individual: his "sentimiento". "Tuvo que desembarcar en Erdosain", he claims, "en el funesto y desdichado Erdosain de 'Los siete locos', que sólo hundiéndose se siente aparecer. Pues –*como equivocamente señalan los que destacan en sus criaturas la influencia de Dostoiewsky*– lo que Arlt, al afrontar el problema general de la vida, descubrió en sí y transmitió a sus personajes, *a semejanza de Dostoiewsky*, fue que los argentinos, los americanos, como los rusos, sienten una especie de ilegalidad vital, una desautorización de sus existencias en el ámbito nacional, como si esa justificación estuviera reservada sólo para el occidente de Europa, una ilegalidad que con la búsqueda de la intensidad del sufrimiento, de los apretujones del dolor, se intenta superar".[13] Murena is a master of the technique of deducing national characteristics from individual cases. His essay on Florencio Sánchez and what he calls "la pugna contra el silencio" is a "tour de force" of this kind of rationalization. Similarly, through his examination of Arlt, he seeks to probe what he sees as certain aspects of Argentine life. However this may be, it is difficult to understand why the fact that Arlt drew direct inspiration from the Russian novelist necessarily detracts from his achievement in an Argentine context. Is it not more feasible that Arlt, starting from his personal experience, perceived in Dostoevsky that the exaltation of suffering and anguish might be the key to the unlocking of the mystery of the life he saw around him?

Arlt's daughter, Mirta, makes more specific a claim for Russian influence. She describes her father's life immediately before the publication of his first novel, when he went to Córdoba and unsuccessfully tried his hand in business. Hard upon his failure, he returned to Buenos Aires at the age of twenty-five. "Trae parte de *El juguete rabioso* escrita. Estamos ya en el año 1925. La revolución rusa, la Tercera Internacional, el arresto de Trotsky en lo político, Tolstoi y Dostoevski en lo literario, son el caldo de cultivo en que alimenta su lucubración".[14] Bernardo Kordón, discussing Dostoevsky's shadow over Arlt, adds weight to this opinion: "...hay pescados que los sacó de Buenos Aires, pero a un montón los pescó en la literatura".[15]

As we said earlier, with more recent work on Arlt, this ghost –shrouded in vague nationalistic assertion– is now duly laid. Many Argentine critics have refused to face the obvious. "La obra de Arlt no pierde su originalidad por eso, sino que crece en importancia por la inusitada forma que el autor argentino dio a los materiales dostoievskianos" says Goštautas. Surely all must now agree with him.[16]

Suffering and "soledad"

In our Introduction we have made brief reference to the theme of *soledad* as a constant in the Argentine novel and short story from the 1920s onwards. In this process, there is no doubt that Mallea has been the main driving force, forging great characters like Agata Cruz or Chaves out of this concept. As we have seen, his first publication dates, like Arlt's, from 1926, with *Cuentos para una inglesa desesperada*, a collection of prose poems containing the seeds of his later work, with its nostalgic evocation of the loneliness of its characters.[17] It lacks the spirit of commitment which was to become characteristic of his work in the 1930s, however, in *Nocturno europeo* or *Historia de una pasión argentina* or the more sophisticated existential ideas on authenticity and communication which lie at the heart of the series of *porteño* stories in *La ciudad junto al río inmóvil*. However, we must guard against the assumption that Mallea was the sole moving force at this time behind the incorporation of this theme into Argentine literature, for he was not alone by any means.[18] During the same period, Arlt's contribution to the exploration of *soledad* is considerable. In *El juguete rabioso*, Silvio's rejection by society and his awareness of his own insufficiency and suffering are sure pointers to the greater importance that this theme was to assume in his next publication in 1929. In the later novels, anguish and humiliation inevitably lead to separation and *soledad*. Admittedly, Arlt never raised the concept to the philosophical level that is normal in Mallea, with whom it becomes an instrument of self-awareness, under the influence of thinkers like Berdyaev and Unamuno. For Arlt, *soledad* is the state which is naturally inherent in the life of the city-dweller in Buenos Aires. All the relationships of the characters in *Los siete locos* and *Los lanzallamas* have as their point of departure a yearning for communication. Erdosain is not only alienated from the body of other urban dwellers but all his relationships with the individual characters in the novels are totally unfulfilled. No fruitful personal communication is ever established in these works, unless it be the one between el Astrólogo and Hipólita. And even on this Arlt hesitates to dwell. As we shall see in the next chapter, when we consider the question of relationships between the sexes, the whole problem of interpersonal contact is one in which the male characters feel constrained to destroy any growing communication with their womenfolk.

At times, Arlt seems to imply certain existential truths that were to be exploited much later by other novelists, in particular that through suffering human beings establish a form of communion. "...los hombres que sufren llegan a conocer idénticas verdades. Hasta pueden decirlas con las mismas palabras", he writes in 1931. We have interpreted the longing for suffering in his works as a masochistic tendency and its converse, the desire to inflict humiliation, as a sadistic one. If we accept Fromm's thesis, we must also conceive of these processes as a striving for some form of communication with others. However, here we are faced by a paradox. As Masotta has pointed out, Arlt, like Dostoevsky, was very well aware that there is no closer relationship than that between executioner and victim (in the literal and metaphorical sense), between humiliator and humiliated. But between humiliated and degraded individuals themselves, no such communication is possible. "Si hay un tema rector en esta obra, hacia donde confluye lo más específicamente arltiano, entiendo que es el de la imposibilidad de contacto entre humillado y humillado".[19] Thus, by an inverse process, there is a tendency in Arlt's novels towards a continual forming of groups, but groups of individuals who have no fundamental communication between them. The first part of *El juguete rabioso* revolves around the experiences of the adolescent gang, "Los Caballeros de la Medianoche", which is a small scale model for the Astrólogo's group of conspirators in the following two books. It is also noteworthy that as the group activity increases, the theme of *soledad* is also more in evidence. So, in *Los lanzallamas*, the alienation of the main characters from each other is much more often alluded to than in its predecessor. Apart from the natural growth in the intensity of the theme as Arlt's writing proceeds, there may well be historical reasons for this phenomenon. Towards the end of the twenties was the moment when existential themes made their real impact on Buenos Aires literature. It is certain, as Stabb indicates, that familiarity with existential philosophy in Buenos Aires dates from the late twenties and that the consequent influence on creative literature was almost immediate.[20] Mallea was about to launch his major work around the concept of *soledad*; Scalabrini published *El hombre que está solo y espera* (a thoroughly existentialist title) in 1931; Arlt brings out *Los lanzallamas* in the same year. By 1932 the review *Sur* was already publishing Heidegger in translation. At all events, apart from the general assumption of Erdosain's alienation, Arlt makes no specific reference to the theme of solitude in *Los siete locos* until the book is well advanced. "El y los otros. Entre él y los otros se interponía una distancia, era quizás la incomprensión de los demás, o quizás su locura. De cualquier forma, no era por eso menos desdichado" [NCC I 254]. However, in *Los lanzallamas*, the theme is specific from the start, as though Arlt had reassessed his philosophical stand from one work to the other. "Estoy monstruosamente solo" laments Erdosain now, immured in the "funeraria soledad de su cuarto".

El tic-tac del reloj suena muy distante. Erdosain cierra los ojos. Lo van aislando del mundo sucesivas envolturas perpendiculares de silencio, que caen fuera de él, una tras otra, con tenue roce de suspiro. Silencio y soledad [NCC II 33].

Está absolutamente solo, entre tres mil millones de hombres y en el corazón de la ciudad [NCC II 34].

Later in the same volume, more dynamic qualitites are attributed to his state of loneliness, as though it paralyzed him, producing psychosomatic symptoms, as it does in Mallea's creative writing.[21]

El problema se afiebra en su interior. Le arden las mejillas y le zumban los oídos. Erdosain comprende que lo que extingue su fuerza es la terrible impotencia de estar solo, de no tener junto a él un alma que recoja su desesperado S.O.S. [NCC II 53].

Elsa's account of their life together is also one of endless silences, sometimes lasting weeks on end. Later Arlt is at pains to render a psychological account of this silence in his character's life, placing its origins yet again in his childhood, as he did with his sense of humiliation. "Remo había vivido casi una infancia aislada", he writes. "Debido a su carácter huraño no podía mantener relaciones con otros chicos de su edad. Rápidamente éstas degeneraban en riñas". He calls him "una criatura taciturna", adding: "El niño insensiblemente se fue acostumbrando a la soledad, hasta que la soledad se le hizo querida" [NCC II 160]. And when Erdosain is visited by the gassed soldier, as in a nightmare, the twin concepts of humiliation and *soledad* are virtually fused into one.

> Padre, padre mío: estoy solo. He estado siempre solo. Sufriendo. ¿Qué tengo que hacer? Me han roto desde chico, padre. Desde que empecé a vivir. Siempre me han roto. A golpes, a humillaciones, a insultos. He sufrido, padre [NCC II 171].

Hitherto, we have had little occasion to refer to Arlt's third novel, *El amor brujo*, as it falls into a different category. We shall be concerned with it in the following chapter. Although its protagonist Estanislao Balder could not be classed as an *angustiado* in the grand manner of the previous novels, he suffers from his own form of isolation. This may be seen as evidence that Arlt had turned a sympathetic ear towards the general tendencies then becoming evident (1931-32). Balder's loneliness first manifests itself as a symptom of his having fallen short of the heroic destiny he would have desired for himself. Arlt uses the device of allowing the character to consider himself a semi-idiot (as with Prince Myshkin), the more clearly to see the people and circumstances around him. He is also an *abúlico* incapable of utilizing his real gifts. In fact, in the novels he shows himself to be a gifted engineer and no mean critic of society. "Dicha semiimbecilidad (de la cual yo tenía conciencia a medias, pues no me pasaba desapercibido que enneblinaba mi vida) aguzó de tal manera mi susceptibilidad, que poco a poco me fui aislando. El trato con mis prójimos me era insoportable". "Cuando tenía que ponerme en contacto con un desconocido, no podía evitar cierta conmoción nerviosa, una hostilidad que a mí mismo se me hacía perceptible en el temblor de los párpados..." [NCC III 45, 46]. Whilst *soledad* is not the generative force in Balder as it is in Erdosain, it nevertheless lies at the heart of his relations with others. He has, admittedly, a passionate and illicit sexual relationship with the schoolgirl Irene, but even this contact is gnawed away by his own doubts and fears of becoming the dupe of her mother and the victim of bourgeois values in marriage. His loneliness, though not insisted on as with the *angustiados* of Arlt's contemporaries, is equally real. "Te hablo" he tells his wife "porque me siento tan solo en la vida como si me encontrara en un desierto". "Me habré quedado solo en el mundo. Solo entre mil quinientos millones de mujeres". "Está solo en el mundo, se siente más débil que una criatura para afrontar el vacío de sus días y de sus noches" [NCC III 124, 125, 140]. Thus, although the concept of *soledad* does not come to occupy the formally dominant position in his writing which it does with some of his contemporaries, it is nevertheless a pervasive force implicit in the situation he creates for his characters and in their behaviour towards each other. In a sense, all Arlt's characters are engaged in an endless monologue directed at those around them; the two-way process is never realized. It is therefore to be underlined how loneliness reasserts itself at the end of *Los lanzallamas*. As Erdosain lies in bed with la Bizca, whose sexual attentions fill him with revulsion, the feeling aroused in him before he commits the final act of murder that will sever his connections with the world is that of his own irremediable solitude, which itself is tantamount to death. La Bizca is trying to arouse his sexual appetite:

> Tristemente la dejaba hacer. Comprendióse más huérfano que nunca en la terrible soledad de la casa de todos, y cerró los ojos con piedad por sí mismo. La vida se le escapaba por los dedos, como la electricidad por las puntas. En este desangramiento, Remo renunció a todo. En él apareció la aceptación de una muerte construida ya con la vida más espantosa que el verídico morir físico [NCC II 249].

Thereupon, he shoots la Bizca by inserting a gun in her ear (phallic symbolism?) and she dies in the most horrific fashion. The way is now open to his own suicide. His loneliness has come full circle.

CHAPTER III

SEXUALITY AND THE SEX WAR

Arlt belonged to the vanguard in Argentina of those writers who were attempting to bring the individual to the centre of the stage, in the wake of the new existential thinking in the 1920s; he was the first to incorporate the theme of existential anguish into his narrative in a bold fashion; he was the first writer in Argentina to introduce the city as a major force in its own right into the novel, thus making a definitive break with the lingering rural tradition in River Plate literature. He also carried fantasy, albeit crudely, to a level hitherto unknown in the Argentine novel, if not throughout Latin America, which was a sure pointer to future developments in the "new novel" in all parts of Spanish America in its flight from telluric themes towards a more urban-based literature. In this area of his work Arlt must now be regarded as an important precursor in a literary rebellion against traditional values and it is presumably for these reasons that writers like Cortázar and Onetti hold him so high in their esteem. It is therefore a curious and signal fact that in the area of his work connected with the role of sex and relations between the sexes (as opposed to sexual relations – hardly anyone has sexual relations in Arlt's writing!) he seems to turn a mirror to the society around him rather than open up any new avenues of thought or creativity. We do not wish to suggest by this that we are dealing with hermetic compartments in his thinking, for there exist strong links between the concepts of anguish and humiliation and the relations between the sexes. What is more important is that whilst Arlt had a great share in hammering out the new concept of the anguished and lonely individual trapped in his urban environment, his view of women (and therefore most of the female characters he created) seems to be governed by traditional Argentine values, if not by traditional *porteño* myths. On the other hand, his view of bourgeois marriage and the institutionalization of sexual relations is aggressive and iconoclastic. These concepts must be kept apart in our analysis, although, as in all Arlt's thinking, they intermingle and play upon each other, making neat definitions difficult to arrive at. For this reason, we shall review briefly the attitudes on which Arlt draws and examine the contemporary background in this respect, before we try to disentangle the ramifications of this problem in his fiction. [1]

Whilst this was a period in which women were fighting for their rights all over the advanced world,[2] a singular attitude subsisted in Latin America, and particularly in Buenos Aires, which has come to be known as *machismo*. The term is common coinage nowadays. It is too simple to write off this attitude as a mere desire for the continuance of male dominance in society, as an attempt simply to keep women "in their proper place". The roots go much deeper in so heterogeneous a society as Buenos Aires and Argentina at large. H. E. Lewald says of the phenomenon:

> Durante las épocas en que la región del Río de la Plata fue tierra fronteriza para los colonizadores y más tarde para los inmigrantes, existió una pronunciada escasez de mujeres. Tal vez el machismo, concepto tan prevalente y discutido en las naciones latinoamericanas, que equivale a un despliegue de coraje desafiante y de fuerza masculina, también se desarrolló en Buenos Aires fomentado por el impulso del hombre solitario. Así se explicaría que, una vez conquistada, la porteña de antaño quedaba encerrada entre cuatro paredes domésticas.[3]

Scalabrini Ortiz, too, was an acute commentator on heterosexual aspects of *porteño* life. Going back to the end of the last century, to what he calls "el peliagudo achaque de la avalancha inmigratoria", he discusses the strong historical reasons for the divisions between the sexes which became a characteristic of life. Firstly, as he says, one must take account of the simple numerical imbalance, since during the early years of immigration, men greatly outweighed women. He writes:

> [Buenos Aires] enclaustró a sus mujeres, ya insuficientes para la compañía de cientos de miles, de millones de hombres que arribaban solos, embarcados en una quimera de hartura corporal. ... Buenos Aires no quería mujeres: las repudiaba, aunque el equilibrio sexual estaba ya seriamente comprometido y en un millón y pico de habitantes había ciento veinte mil mujeres menos que hombres. ... Por la presión del ambiente enrarecido, la mujer veía en el hombre al timador de su honestidad. El hombre en la mujer, la enemiga de su lozanía instintiva. Los hombres quedaron desamparados.[4]

This second paragraph might serve as an accurate résumé of the attitude assumed by Arlt's male characters towards their relationships with women – as necessary but dangerous and intrusive. According to Scalabrini, this situation had the inevitable result of sacrificing all normal, gentle relations between the sexes. All forms of *camaradería* were banished. Men who frequented women (other than in a spirit of conquest, presumably) came to be seen as unfaithful to their male relationships and thought of as *maricón* or "*caliente*". "(El Hombre de Corrientes y Esmeralda) no tuvo camaradas del otro sexo, 'tuvo programas', presas que cayeron en el lazo; mujeres sonsacadas, víctimas, frutos de su destreza, de su 'muñeca', verdaderos actos de pillaje, demostraciones de arrojo o astucia."[5]

To compound this situation and largely because of it, Buenos Aires became the city of rampant prostitution and the infamous *trata de blancas*.[6] Without some knowledge of the degrading conditions to which the city had sunk by 1925, when Arlt began to write seriously, it is quite impossible to understand the creation of characters like the Rufián Melancólico (a travesty of Cervantes's "El rufián dichoso", of course), with his sadistic exploitation of the women he keeps or the proposals to finance the revolution by a chain of brothels. This is, indeed, the Rufián's task in the revolutionary group, to organize the brothels. Carella describes the whorehouses of this period in picturesque terms:

> Había prostíbulos de dos tipos: individuales y colectivos. No siempre respondían a la calificación de proxeneta minorista y mayorista. El negocio era complicado. El amo de una esclava podía hacerla trabajar sola o entre muchas que no le pertenecían. En la ciudad se permitían los individuales. El instalarlo era cosa sencilla pues sólo se necesitaba una vivienda. La puta ocupaba dos habitaciones para su trabajo. En tanto que un cliente servido completaba su tocado después del acto, ella atendía a otro cliente en la alcoba próxima. La actividad sincronizada rendía más dinero en menos tiempo. En el vestíbulo había sillas para los que aguardaban turno.[7]

(Arlt's character Erdosain frequently sits on one of these chairs, in an advanced state of anguish.) Albert Londres states that the price of a French girl –price to *buy*, that is!– was about 30,000 French francs, the rent of premises 700 or 800 pesos per month.[8] His conversations with pimps operating at the time, in 1928, when Arlt was composing *Los siete locos*, are most revealing and confirm Arlt's social realism in this respect. After some four or five years' work, a pimp might hope to retire with some fifteen hundred thousand francs. A girl "who unlaced her sandal", as he puts it so delicately, from thirty to thirty-five times a day was thought to be a good worker. Elsewhere, he quotes the unbelievable figure of seventy to seventy-five, "at certain seasons" (!).[9] Carella bears this out when he says: "A veces era posible ver a una pecadora enardeciendo a tres, cuatro y hasta cinco candidatos al mismo tiempo".[10] The peculiarity of the trade in Buenos Aires was the *macró*[11] or *canfinflero*, who maintained one or more women and exploited them individually himself or in common premises. Carella states that in the year of the Centenario (1910) thirty-seven per cent of women in Buenos Aires were involved in prostitution and that seventy-five per cent of all crimes were due to them. These figures may be open to doubt but there is no gainsaying the magnitude of the problem. Suicides were frequent and venereal disease and tuberculosis were rampant at the time Arlt was a young adolescent. Little wonder that prostitution and brothels figure so heavily in his fiction. Prostitution remained legal until 1936 when the law changed.

The social condition of women in Buenos Aires during this period was not only one of inferiority but fraught, too, with economic distress, which was to be aggravated by the depression from 1929 onwards. Arlt admirably captures this moment of social stress in his *Aguafuertes* with his sketches of working-class women making ends meet by taking in washing and sewing. In his novels and stories, however, he is concerned with characters from the lower middle class where, if anything, the situation was even worse. As Arturo Jauretche points out, the women of the middle class were denied access to the menial solutions adopted by their social inferiors, their only possibility lying in teaching or matrimony.[12] Against this background the behaviour of Arlt's Hipólita becomes much clearer.

A further reflection of the relations between the sexes may be found in the popular tangos of the period, in which the scheming woman is often depicted as the instrument of man's downfall, usually at the expense of his filial duties to his mother. The concept of woman as treacherous in love is a basic assumption of *El amor brujo* (whence the title) and a number of Arlt's stories display the *novia* invariably in league with her scheming mother, to the detriment of the man who is set up as the victim (or *gil* as he is known in *lunfardo*). This is a popular basis of many tangos, going hand in hand with male reticence and *machismo*. One of the best-known tangos is *La cumparsita* by Pascual Contursi. Its words run as follows:

Abandonó/a su viejita/que quedó desamparada,/
y loco de pasión,/ ciego de amor/corrió/
tras su amada/ que era linda, era hechicera,/
de lujuria era una flor/y burló su querer/
hasta que se cansó/ y por otro lo dejó./
Largo tiempo/después, cayó al hogar/materno.[13]

The great master of the tango, Enrique Santos Discépolo, writes in "Secreto": "¿Quién sos/ que no puedo salvarme/ muñeca maldita,/ castigo de Dios?" The girl is repeatedly seen as "traicionera" and "ingrata". In a very famous tango by Diego Flores, "Copetín, vos sos mi hermano", we come across: "Mas la vida es justiciera/ y la ingrata la ha de ver/ como yo, triste y llorando,/ y por la vida arrastrando/ sus orgullos de mujer." Such examples might easily be multiplied but these few lines will show to what extent Arlt's idea of the "novia traicionera" is a reflection of a widespread undercurrent in the *porteño* atmosphere of his day, the vital difference being that in Arlt's fiction the males usually take the initiative and sever their relationship with the girl before they can be deceived. The image of the treacherous woman remains the same, however, throughout his fiction. This is in no way at variance with his other concept of the purity of women, as "señoritas", as we saw when dealing with Erdosain's psychological development. They are merely two sides of the same coin and accord with the general motive force in Arlt's work: the aspiration to purity frustrated by wordly realities.

It might be useful at this point to take up an observation made by Mafud about the role of women characters in Argentine fiction. He states that women never achieve status in the novel and that their basic trait is impersonality. With particular regard to Arlt, he contends, quite rightly, that they are violently absorbed by their male counterparts, not even excepting the compelling character Hipólita, who, whilst resisting any relationship with Erdosain, falls into the vortex of the Astrólogo's influence at the end. Mafud claims that the male-orientated society in Argentina has not changed to this day. Although women may have an apparently greater equality, he says, "su visión es la misma. Es la de su madre o su abuela. Posee la misma culpa en sus actos o en sus gestos. Aunque hoy sea camarada, compañera o salga en grupo, actúa movida por los mismos tabús y el mismo temor."[14] (He was writing at the end of the 1950s.)

Let us turn again to Arlt, in the hope that these brief introductory remarks may provide a background against which to set his ideas on sex and sexual relations into perspective. They are often grotesque and they have given offence to many women readers – and they have often been misunderstood.

A theory of relationships between the sexes

Arlt's approach to relationships between the sexes bears the stamp of the contemporary view of woman as the enemy of man's "lozanía instintiva", but it is complicated by the recurrent theme of the purity of woman. We have said that these are two sides of the same coin, one having its origin in machismo and social conditions, the other deriving from the general pursuit of an ideal which is apparent in his humiliated characters. For purposes of definition, we shall try to keep these two areas apart, although they inevitably react one on the other. It would be foolhardy to suggest that Buenos Aires invented machismo; man's sense of domination and his fear of woman as the destroyer of his liberty and inhibiter of his aspirations is presumably as old as the institution of marriage. Machismo may be construed as a manifestation of this fear. It is an idea which has remained vigorous throughout Spanish literature and art, from the Celestina onwards, in which woman as the agent of man's downfall is a major theme. Indeed, the theme has its very roots in the Bible. One has only to turn to Quevedo, who clearly had some influence over the development of Arlt's style (particularly in the Aguafuertes), to test its strength. Woman as the enemy of man's purse and person is a mainspring of Quevedo's writing. Similarly, it is a standard acceptance in Goya's drawings (Los caprichos) that man is a ready victim of woman's wiles.[15]

A consideration of this aspect of Arlt's writing carries us into El amor brujo and the stories published in El jorobadito, in which sexual relations are consistently interpreted as a snare. However, the theme is broached in one or two instances in the earlier works, which call for immediate investigation, for they are a key to his later thinking. In Los siete locos,

Hipólita is the only character, apart from Erdosain, who is permitted the indulgence of exploring her own psychological state. Like him, she has suffered when young, been humiliated and experienced grave loneliness. Contrary to the other characters, most of whom are failed professional people, she appears to be of working-class origin. She has been a serving-maid in a wealthy household and this position has isolated her from the world: "...a momentos me parecía que los otros estaban clavados en la vida, y en sus casas, mientras que yo tenía la sensación de estar suelta, ligeramente atada con un cordón a la vida. Y las voces de los otros sonaban en mis oídos como cuando una está dormida y no sabe si sueña o está despierta" [NCC I 331]. She describes the first stirrings of her sexual awareness but, unlike the male characters, proceeds rapidly to the solution of her anguished condition *by means of sex*. She had once heard a young man on a tram propounding the hypothesis that an intelligent woman, even an ugly one, might become wealthy by taking up "la mala vida" and, provided she never fell in love, become "la reina de la ciudad". (Such a notion is quite feasible in the Buenos Aires of those days, as we have noted.) In the disconcerting way that Arlt's characters have of tackling their problems head on, she spends her next month's wages buying books about "la mala vida", but these merely turn out to be pornographic. "...ésa no era la mala vida" she says "sino la mala vida del placer". After visiting the law-courts to see if the truth is to be found there, she finally consults a doctor-of-laws. From him she ascertains, paradoxically, that by performing acts of love, purely for profit, she will be capable of liberating herself from her own body. More important than this theoretical discovery is her first sexual experience, from which she soon learns that a woman may exert total domination over a man through the sexual act; that a man, who at first seemed impregnable as a fortress, falls like a felled steer on achieving satisfaction. Thenceforward, she seeks a "lion" amongst men, whom she may admire. But all men fail her, save the Astrólogo. With him she achieves final satisfaction *because* he is castrated! The scene in *Los lanzallamas* in which he reveals his livid scar to her is a moment of great truth. "Sos ... el único hombre" she cries. Whilst it is possible to interpret this as typical of Arlt's penchant for black humour, it nevertheless provides a serious basis on which to judge his thinking about sex, from which we see that copulation is degrading to man, robbing him of his virility and leading to his ultimate domination by the female.

Maldavsky purports to see in Arlt a strong Oedipus complex which he claims is manifest in this aspect of his thought; he calls it "la denigración del coito excluyente".[16] He affirms that castration anxieties predominate in Arlt over attraction to the opposite sex. What is certain is that there is a link in the novels between the drive towards sexual purity, which is merely a part of the general urge in Arlt's characters to discover ideals and absolutes, and the frustration of the latter by the reality upon which they stumble. In this way, the anguish aroused in Erdosain by his sexual dissatisfaction must be seen as an important factor in his derangement rather than the main reason for it, as Maldavsky would imply.

A natural corollary of the tendency to see women as dominating man through sex is the attack on marriage as its end-product; that is, marriage as institutionalized amongst the middle classes. It is in this area that the male characters' fears are constantly exposed and it is here, too, that *machismo*, or at least its handmate, the fear of domination, may be seen at its most virulent. It is first hinted at in *Los lanzallamas* when Erdosain meets la Bizca and her mother. The latter is the first in a series of potential mother-in-law figures who not only strike terror into the male protagonists but are repulsive creatures in their own right. In a spirit of mockery, Erdosain proposes to establish relations with María la Bizca. This becomes possible because her mother has her eyes on the large quantity of money given to Erdosain by the Astrólogo. Protesting the while about her daughter's innocence and tender years and her own family lineage, she prepares to sell out. Arlt's description of her is typical of the many to follow and speaks of a deep-seated hatred of the sham that such individuals represent.

> Silenciosamente entró doña Ignacia. Era una mujer alta, gruesa, de cara redonda y paperas. Su negro cabello anillado, y ojos muertos como los de un pez, unido a la prolongada caída del vértice de los labios, le daba el aspecto de mujer cruel y sucia. En torno del cuello llevaba una cinta de terciopelo negro. Unas zapatillas rotas desaparecían bajo el ruedo de su batón de cuadros negros y blancos abultado extraordinariamente sobre los pechos. Soslayó el dinero, y pasando la lengua ávidamente por el borde de los labios lustrosos dijo: –Señor Erdosain... [NCC II 36].

Such are the gruesome mothers who live vicariously through their daughters, guiding their every action to help them trap their man. (She is a widow, of course.) Arlt makes quite explicit this vicarious relationship later in the novel. Erdosain walks out with la Bizca, who shows off her pointed breasts and sports a skirt "que, a la menor presión del viento, dejaba ver las puntilladas ligas a los tenderos" [NCC II 188]. (It is once again the shopkeepers who are the butt of his scorn, just as much as the action of the girl.) La Bizca neither loves him nor has any respect for him; she merely reacts to the social forces canalized through the mother. "Apenas si lo estimaba, pero los largos considerandos de su madre, que no pensaba en ella, la persuadieron de tal manera que si Erdosain la hubiera abandonado la muchacha habría sufrido lo indecible. Erdosain constituía para ella lo inmediato, es decir, el eterno marido" [NCC II 187].[17] As Masotta points out, these mothers represent the instrument through which, generation after generation, society perpetuates itself.[18] So, in *El amor brujo*, Irene's mother, Señora Loayza, maintains the same draconian control over her daughter, the difference being that this later novel has the problem of sexual relations and marriage as its major theme and the relationship between the male and female characters is even more ambiguous than in the previous works. There are effectively two couples in the novel: Irene and Balder (unmarried)[19] and Zulema and Alberto (married). In each case, the men are finally deceived: Balder by Irene who maintained that she was a virgin, when she was not, and Alberto by Zulema, who sleeps with her dancing instructor. All four are made to waltz around the *éminence grise* of the novel, Señora Loayza. It is an oversimplification to state that Balder is deceived for, like all Arlt's male characters, he suspends the relationship before a final grave situation is reached. The novel is kept alive by his vacillation about Irene's supposed double-dealings and whether her sensuality is sincere or promoted from the background by her scheming mother. Unlike the case of la Bizca's mother, in *El amor brujo* the issue is never resolved and doubt is one of the important sub-themes of the work. Indeed, although it is mainly concerned with relationships between the sexes, the problem of doubt and the inability of Balder to achieve any firm knowledge about other persons' motives, or even about his own, is raised to quasi-philosophical levels. There even appears a character called El Fantasma de la Duda.

Before examining Arlt's view of marriage in detail, we must look back to the associated problem of the search for purity in heterosexual relations, for the one is a key to the other. We were obliged in our previous analysis of the origin of anguish in Erdosain to consider his sexual insufficiency, along with other causes. We saw how he believed that a man married "para estar siempre junto a su mujer y gozar la alegría de verse a todas horas", that young women were not to be kissed, nor even addressed as *tú*, and how on his wedding night he had gone to bed with his trousers on. It is not necessary to reopen this problem, but we must enlarge upon it in order to understand Arlt's view of marriage which colours a large part of his writing. In a scene in which Erdosain is travelling on an electric train, he recalls an earlier meeting with Ergueta, who had shown him a photograph of Hipólita, the prostitute he intends to marry in order to "save" her. Hipólita seems to represent the ideal of womanhood in Arlt's world. Not only has she inquired into the meaning of life and overcome her body through prostitution but she aspires to a higher plane of existence. This is how she is described:

Ella no sonreía. A sus espaldas los espacios estaban abigarrados de palmas y helechos. Sentada en un banco con la cabeza ligeramente inclinada, miraba una revista que su rodilla sostenía, pues cruzaba una pierna sobre otra. De esta forma, a poca distancia del césped, el vuelo de su vestido suspendía una campana. El alto peinado y los cabellos huídos de sus sienes hacían más clara y ancha la luna de su frente. A los lados de la fina nariz, el arco de las cejas era delgado como conviene a los ojos que son ligeramente oblicuos en un rostro delicadamente ovalado [NCC I 313].

It is not necessary to analyse this passage in detail (with its displaced epithets, suggestive adverbs and romantic background) to realise that Hipólita is grossly idealized. Moreover, there is an interesting detail, apart from the gentleness of her features which is absent from almost all other female characters; the way her skirt forms around her body. This seems to have been a visual fixation with Arlt. The other woman much idealized in his writing is Ester Primavera who is also identified by the same detail. "El vestido negro se atorbellinaba en torno de sus piernas ágiles...". They also share the same hair: "los cabellos huídos de las sienes..."; "un bucle de cabellos dejábale libre la sien...". However, the significant fact is Erdosain's puritanical reaction to Hipólita in the photograph (bearing in mind she is a prostitute): "Y mirándola, Erdosain supo de pronto que junto a Hipólita él no experimentaría jamás ningún deseo..." [NCC I 313]. Later in the novel, when he meets her in person, although they reveal their innermost thoughts to each other within hours, their relationship remains quite platonic. They sleep in the same room, exhausted by the mutual revelation of their anguished lives, Erdosain having spent hours with his head on her lap; but there is no sexual contact; they repudiate the flesh, as Arlt puts it. On another occasion, Luciana Espila offers herself to Erdosain, who brusquely refuses her. Not in a mood of disdain, however. "Me he desvestido para hacerte el regalo de mi cuerpo", she tells him. "No quiero que sigas sufriendo." But Erdosain's mind wanders to another creature, in an ideal landscape, to a young girl he has seen but once and never met. "Efectivamante, sos muy linda" he says to Luciana, but he will not touch her. Suffering is not to be assuaged in his case by sexual contact, simply because suffering of this kind is the product of unfulfilled ideals. His frequenting of brothels thus not only increases his anguish but serves to cut him off more deeply still from the rest of mankind. Berdyaev has devoted careful attention to this aspect of sex, in which woman becomes part of the objective world instead of a communicant in a person-to-person relationship. He writes in *Solitude and Society*: "the physical union between the sexes, which puts an end to sexual desire, is not in itself sufficient to banish solitude. Indeed, it may intensify man's sense of solitude."[20] The longing for an ideal of purity is explicitly stated by Erdosain to Hipólita:

> – No sé ... muchas veces pensaba en la pureza ... yo hubiera querido ser un hombre puro –y entusiasmándose, continuó–: Muchas veces sentí la tristeza de no ser hombre puro. ¿Por qué? No lo sé. Pero ¿se imagina usted un hombre de alma blanca enamorado por vez primera ... y que todos fueran iguales? ¿Se imagina usted qué amor enorme entre una mujer pura y un hombre puro? Entonces, antes de entregarse el uno al otro, se matarían ... o no; sería ella la que se ofrecería a él ... luego se suicidarían, comprendiendo la inutilidad de vivir sin ilusiones [NCC I 334].

(Would it be exaggerating a point to see in this very statement the ambivalence of Arlt's –or, at least, his character's– attitude in the deft transition from "entregarse el uno al otro" to "sería ella la que se ofrecería a él"? Or is this once again Arlt mocking the susceptibility of his own characters?)

As Arlt sees it, then, it is precisely for these reasons that bourgeois marriage, since it institutionalizes and destroys such ideals, is a subject for scorn. At the best of times, he lambasts the pennypinching mentality of the middle class; but marriage amongst the bourgeois invokes his direct wrath.[21] It is noticeable that this theme increases in frequency from *Los siete locos* to *Los lanzallamas* until it takes pride of place in *El amor brujo*. In the second of these works, Erdosain imagines himself married to la Bizca, with all the horrendous social implications that this might entail. His anger has splenetic overtones and, at times, assumes disgusting proportions.

> Se imaginó casada con la Bizca. La revé en una casa de inquilinato, desventrada y gorda, leyendo entre flato y flato alguna novela que le ha presentado la carbonera de la esquina. Holgazana como siempre, si antes era abandonada ahora descuida por completo su higiene personal, emporcando con sus menstruaciones sábanas que nunca se resuelve a lavar. Tendrían algún hijo, eso era lo más probable, y a la mesa, mientras que la criatura, con el traserito enmerdado, berreaba tremendamente, ella le contaría alguna pelea con una vecina, reproduciendo todas sus frases atroces e injurias imposibles. Y el pueril motivo de la pelea habría sido el robo de un puñadito de sal o la utilización indebida de una cuerda de colgar ropa [NCC II 188].

Such is the bitter dish, says Arlt, of the city-bound employee, of "los hombres que viven de su sueldo y que tienen un jefe". It must surely be seen that such loathing can only be the product of a failure to come to terms with the sordid reality of life on the one hand and impossible ideals on the other. What is certain is that Arlt's revulsion at the demands of conventional marriage, tied to the daily impositions of urban life, –"el desastre cotidiano de un millón ochocientos mil habitantes que tiene la ciudad"– gives rise to some of his most nauseous pages. This is the tone that invests *El amor brujo*, not only in its overall theme, which is based on the betrayal of human values by social ones, but in its strident attack on middle-class marriage. Balder's whole endeavour is to avoid becoming a *gil* (a dupe or easy victim), to escape the fate of millions around him, to become singular and shun the anonymity of the mass.

Let us now examine the view of marriage expressed in this last novel, for it provides a clue to the way in which the narrative develops. In fact, given such hatred of middle-class conventions, *El amor brujo* could end in one way only, – in separation and disruption. Whilst in *Los lanzallamas* the attack on marriage is vituperative and mindless, here there is an advance towards more sociologically-based analysis. Having decided that his main theme was to be sex and marriage, Arlt seems to have determined to make his argument watertight. Thus the work contains long passages of painful but more objective comment on the attitudes of middle-class women. (Nowhere does he attack male values of *hombría* and *machismo*. The man is always a potential victim. Arlt's criticism of the male bourgeois always relates to his petty materialism, of which the *tendero* is the prime and constant example.) Firstly, he is specific about the women he is discussing. They belong to the lower middle class ("el grado inmediato que antecede a la mediana burguesía") and to the generation born about 1900; that is, his own. Moreover, a further advance on the previous novel, their attitudes are now seen as a product of their circumstance. Formerly, the bourgeois woman was envisaged as wilfully and individually destructive of men; now she forms part of a group. "La conciencia de ellas estaba estructurada por la sociedad que las había deformado en la escuela, y como las hormigas o las abejas que no se niegan al sacrificio más terrible, satisfacían las exigencias del espíritu grupal. Pertenecían a la generación del año 1900" [NCC III 56]. Or yet again: "Encadenadas por escrúpulos que la educación burguesa les había incrustado en el entendimiento, lo soñaban todo, sin ser capaces, por pusilanimidad, de tomar nada" [NCC II 57]. An understandable condensation takes place in Arlt's thinking following the publication of *Los siete locos*, from 1929 onwards. This is the moment of great crisis in Argentine and world economics. The whole range of his ideology becomes more specific, both in political and social values. He never achieves the completeness of a system, however, nor does he ever dominate total clarity of expression. ("El método de razonar de Arlt es sencillo, sordo y difuso" comments Masotta.)[22] But it may be seen from the above quotations that his point of view had by now taken on a more social orientation: women's attitudes are governed by the society in which they live. This marks a shift towards dialectical materialist principles, of course. Vituperation also gives way temporarily to deeper understanding, even to the extent of recognizing the denial of women's rights. "Vivían en monotonía" he writes, "de la misma manera que sus maridos. La diferencia consistía en que ellas no disfrutaban de ningún derecho" [NCC III 57]. They are the women whose brothers and *novios* are employees or in trade. They live in houses –note the specific sociological detail once again– "cuya fachada se podía confundir con el frente de viviendas ocupadas por familias de la mediana burguesía". Or again: "A la calle salían vestidas correctamente. En ciertas circunstancias, un portero no habría podido individualizar a la semiburguesa de la aristócrata..." [NCC III 57]. The aspiration that all had in common was to be married, whilst the objective of their menfolk was to deceive other women and make a good marriage later. One wonders whether Arlt had read Scalabrini's treatment of the same themes? It seems almost certain; *El hombre que está solo y espera* had quite a success in 1931; Arlt published *El amor brujo* in 1932. It would be hazardous to draw firm conclusions but the parallels are clearly there. At all events, new sociological observations are now being made, neater definitions drawn, closer scrutiny practised, and Arlt benefits from this.

> Dicha etapa de la civilización argentina, comprendida entre el año 1900 y 1930, presenta fenómenos curiosos. Las hijas de tenderos estudian literatura futurista en la Facultad de Filosofía y Letras, se avergüenzan de la roña de sus padres y por la mañana regañan a la criada si en la cuenta del almacén descubren diferencia de centavos. Constamos así la aparición de una democracia (aparentemente muy brillante) que ha heredado íntegramente las raídas mezquindades del destripaterrones o criado tipo y que en su primera y segunda generación, ofrece los subtipos de los hombres de treinta años presentes: individuos insaciados, groseros, torpes, envidiosos y ansiosos de apurar los placeres que barruntan los ricos [NCC III 61].[23]

We must also remember that Arlt was reviewing the social situation from within, without the benefit of hindsight. His picture of the lower middle class is necessarily one-sided, for it is designed to support his thesis about sex and marriage in his novel, which ultimately makes no pretence of objectivity. Looking back from 1967, Jauretche paints an equally depressing picture of the same poverty-stricken middle classes of the year 1930, but on a wider canvas. The Army was refusing thousands of young men as unfit, he says; the most dreaded word of the year was "neumotórax";[24] teachers were without employment and those that had work were often unpaid. "El dolor se combina con la picaresca para sobrevivir. Buenos Aires se puebla de buscavidas y de oficios inverosímiles. Porteños y provincianos hundidos en la desdicha se hacen buscones."[25] Reading Jauretche's description, one realises why marriage had become something of a lifebelt for the young middle-class woman and why Arlt's characters struggle so violently to avoid absorption into the mass. It is to his credit that, equally harassed by these rough economic conditions, he nevertheless found the resilience to condemn the (understandable) bourgeois sense of materialism and its instinct for self-preservation. "–¿Qué debe hacerse? ... ¿Lo grave es que mirando en redor no se descubre nada más que mentiras, y la gente se habituó de tal modo a ellas, que cualquier verdad, incluso la más inocente y accesible, les parece una injuria a las buenas costumbres" [NCC III 59].

Having established the quasi-scientific premise for his argument, his inherent nausea and spleen force their way to the surface again. Balder regards marriage itself as a lie and the family home as a pigsty. "Hombres y mujeres constituían hogares basados en mentiras permanentes" he claims. "El hogar es una mentira. Existe nada más que de nombre. Substancialmente, lo que se define por hogar es una pocilga en la cual un macho, respetablemente denominado esposo, practica los vicios más atroces sin que una hembra, su respetable esposa, se dé por enterada" [NCC III 60]. Finally nausea gives way to compassion. He seems to realize something of the crushing conditions under which the *porteño* was living and he perceives the spiritual problem as paramount. The middle class has lost all sense of hope –"no creían en la felicidad"– and the workers below them survived on one overriding idea, that of becoming middle class themselves. Balder, in a final attack of gall, is described as "uno de los tantos tipos que denominamos 'hombre casado'. Haragán, escéptico, triste."

   Given this view of marriage in the middle class and Arlt's desire to hold it up to scorn, it was unlikely that *El amor brujo* could become a successful novel. It is too closely tied to its times, the circumstantial material is too insistent and, unlike the other novels, it is dated. Balder, like the others, is an anguished character, but the overwhelmingly social origins of his anguish are in sharp contrast with the metaphysical anguish of Erdosain. His failed marriage, his meeting with a young schoolgirl on a train and the impossibility of any outcome of his affair are too slender a framework for a worthwhile comment on society. Arlt had thought to introduce an underlying irony at the beginning of the novel by inflating the euphoria that Balder experiences following his first meeting with the adolescent Irene and setting it against the ugly realities of bourgeois life and the threat that his relationship with the young girl constitutes to his integrity and manhood. But parts of the works slide into a maudlin novelette style and it is saved only by its lengthy examination of social *mores* and by his nauseated reaction to what he suspects to be the trap laid by Irene and her mother. It is probably most valuable for its documentation of one peculiar aspect of a society in the throes of economic distress, taking refuge in the proven means of survival.

   Like Erdosain and Silvio, Balder is motivated by his sense of lost purity and by his striving to believe that the world cannot really be as black as it seems.[26] "Sí, yo sé lo que le pasa a usted" Alberto tells him. "Tiene un concepto idealista de la pureza. Se olvida de que las mujeres tienen necesidades y piensan como los hombres" [NCC III 192]. There is also an admixture of the problem of doubt and uncertainty of knowledge and the impossibility of achieving surety in human relationships, clearly an offshoot of the anti-positivist thinking of the times. "¿Cómo deslindar la verdad entre este cúmulo atroz de apariencias, pruebas y contrapruebas?" But this theme is never adequately elaborated. Arlt employs the diary technique to investigate the shifting sands of the protagonist's mind, groping for some measure of assurance in his life, but the psychological profundity of the previous novels is lacking. Indeed, therein lies the lack of success of *El amor brujo*. Whilst the author's technique in handling his material has visibly improved and whilst certain isolated passages are brilliantly composed, the work lacks the dynamism of the earlier novels because, ill-advisedly, he had moved away from existential anguish, in which he excelled, towards a more socially based criticism, in which his knowledge was too diffuse. Both elements are present in each of his novels but the different emphasis in *El amor brujo* accounts for the plummeting of the tone. His first efforts were being made in the theatre at the same time, concentrating on developing the theme already latent in the previous works, – the clash between the characters' dreams and the sordidness of the world around them. *El amor brujo* had begun to take him in a false direction and he abandoned the novel altogether.

We have now traced the two major tendencies in Arlt's thinking on sexuality and heterosexual relations: man as the prey of woman, in or out of marriage, and woman as the ideal, the personification of purity. Clearly, the frightening mother-in-law figures belong to the first category of predators, although their influence is exerted in a vicarious fashion, whilst the idealized young women (sometimes girls even) belong wholly to the second. The remaining women have a foot in both camps. We saw how Mafud complained that women never achieve real status in Argentine fiction, Arlt included. However, it is not only to the fact that his novels are composed from a uniquely male point of view that the women owe their lack of substance, for they are intentionally projected into the male protagonists' lives in different ways at different times. As predators they are weak characters indeed. (There are no "doña Bárbaras" in Arlt's writing.) But, because they represent the social tendency to perpetuate institutions, they in their turn become the victims of the men. No woman in Arlt's fiction successfully subjugates her man; in every case the woman is abandoned. Manhood and liberty are invariably safeguarded at the expense of the female, whether she is guilty of laying snares or not. To see this merely as Arlt's tacit support for the male cause –which many of his female readers have done– is too simple a view, for there is evidence for a more elaborate understanding of the problem. Apart from the major instance of Balder's repudiation of Irene, because of her supposed lie about her virginity,[27] there are a number of cases in his writing of the deliberate rupture of relations between men and women. This is a very different problem from that of reticence or refusal to enter into a relationship, as happens with Hipólita or Luciana Espila, although they have a similar cause: the resistance to betrayal of the ideal of feminine purity and the supposed degradation induced by sexual contact. Maldavsky has commented acutely on this problem, applying psychological techniques: "En la medida en que el vínculo genital es considerado fuertemente destructivo, los personajes lo rehúyen, y es así como ninguno de ellos aparece descripto en la realización de un coito. Si para los personajes de

Arlt el coito es tan destructivo, esto se debe a que lo han convertido en el equivalente intrapsíquico que tiene lugar cuando fracasan todas las tentativas de externalizar el conflicto: el coito llevaría al estallido del yo, tal como se observa en el caso de Erdosain."[28] Such an argument is applicable both to the failure to establish relations and to the need to break off an existing liaison before sexual contact can be achieved. The cases where the male intentionally abandons the female are as follows: Balder with Irene in *El amor brujo*; the unnamed protagonist in "El jorobadito"; Ricardo Stepens in "Noche terrible" and the narrator in "Ester Primavera". Let us look at each in turn, in search of a recognizable pattern.

El amor brujo is naturally the most sophisticated, being a full-length novel. Arlt uses the vagaries of the sexual situation to explore the ebb and flow of Balder's mind. The story-line is concerned with sex and the sexual attraction of an adolescent for an older man (as in Nabokov's *Lolita*), but an important underlying theme is the fallibility and precariousness of human reason in the apprehension of conflicting evidence. Arlt's curiosity in wishing to investigate a character in the grip of a consuming passion may be appreciated from his statement at the beginning of the book: "El hombre, en cualquier extremo de la pasión, es un espectáculo extraordinario, si sus confesiones permiten delinear la estructura de la misma" [NCC III 42]. Balder is the classic anti-hero, vacillating in his own mind, cut off from society, unable to affirm his own existence; the *abúlico* par excellence. The meeting with Irene and his ensuing passion is the force applied to his circumstance to set the novel in motion, to allow the reader to explore the vicissitudes of his psychology as his reason grapples unsuccessfully with this new element in his life. In spite of its relative failure as a novel, this work is an obvious forerunner of Sábato's *El túnel*. Balder, engineer and architect, isolated, meets Irene and is infatuated; after a long struggle in which evidence and reasoning dance around each other, he severs the connection with the one person who might have given some meaning to his life. In Sábato's work, Castel, a painter, equally isolated, meets María Iribarne and, after a similar process involving the failure of his own reason, finally murders her, thus cutting himself off once again from mankind. She had been the only person in the world who had understood his paintings and he deliberately destroys her. Arlt uses the passionate relationship to mount an attack on bourgeois marriage, a social comment which is quite absent from Sábato's work, of course. Like Sábato in *Sobre héroes y tumbas*, he thrusts his character into a subhuman, subterranean world of nightmarish proportions. (The common denominator is naturally Dostoievski's *Notes*, once again.) In his desire for humiliation at the hands of Irene and her mother, Balder longs to enter into what he calls "el camino tenebroso y largo".

Balder se imaginaba el camino tenebroso como un subsuelo planetario. Avanzaba sinuoso bajo los cimientos de las ciudades terrestres. A veces había casas y otras veces estrellas. Aquel camino iluminado oblicuamente por un sol torcido estaba cortado por callejones de tinieblas más altos que palacios faraónicos. Allí avanzaba a tientas una humanidad de larvas densas, entre espesores alternativos de luz y sombra. Las almas giraban como peonzas, chocaban ayuntándose en cohabitación transitoria, y luego se apartaban para chocar con otros sexos [NCC III 109].

Arlt insists several times on this concept of "un subsuelo humano" or "el subsuelo donde se movían las larvas". (It is difficult to avoid the conclusion that he has also exercized a strong influence over the creation of Sábato's "Informe sobre ciegos" in *Sobre héroes y tumbas*, with its subterranean world, peopled by loathesome creatures.)

As Balder allows himself to be sucked further and further into the morass of his relationships with Irene, the motives behind his actions become clearer. It is identical to that which afflicted Erdosain: to discover what will happen to his soul when pursued to the limits of its endurance. "Yo no tengo miedo que me rompa. Por el contrario. Deseo que ella me tome como un trapo y me retuerza. Y entonces cantaré la gloria" [NCC III 128]. Arlt refers to his character as one who "se aislaba voluntariamente en su pocilga. La pocilga era un pecado, un delito, una actitud, un salto, la permanencia en algún suceso que el alma repudiaba extensamente" [NCC III 110]. If he had been forewarned about the "millones de minutos de sufrimiento" that lay before him, he would not have retreated from his desire to be dominated in his passion. The masochistic dualism of his nature is patently revealed: "¿Por qué anhelo la pureza y me revuelco en la porquería?" he asks himself. Ultimately, his desire for purity and his fear of final surrender, allied to his inability to discover firm knowledge of whether he is the victim of a trap or not, force him into the typical Arltian solution: the severance of the connection. This is the only instance in all Arlt's fiction where copulation is known to have taken place, although it is not described. Balder purports to have discovered that Irene was not a virgin but a young woman "interiorizada por completo en la técnica del placer". He therefore abandons her in a spirit of self-justification. The technical reasons for her abandonment are to be found in *machismo*; a man who values his honour would not marry a sullied woman. But the deeper psychological causes are the valid ones: coitus has destroyed all hope of idealization, contact with reality has shattered all possible illusions.

In the short stories, because of their dimension, no case is elaborated to the same extent as that of Balder, but the same inverse correlation between idealization and sexual contact is always to the fore. If one compares "Noche terrible" with "Ester Primavera", the most striking difference is the cynical view that Stepens takes of Julia's intentions and the wholly idealized picture that the narrator paints of Ester. This distinction may be interpreted in the light of our hypothesis. Between Stepens and Julia sexual contact is well advanced but coitus has not apparently taken place. Julia is therefore seen in the most contemptuous light. "Stepens, sardónico, adivina el curso de los pensamientos de la mujer, y se dice: 'Julia se casaría conmigo aunque fuera un asesino' " [NCC III 339]. Compare the idealization of Ester in the other story: "¡Ester Primavera! Su nombre amontona pasado en mis ojos. Mis sobresaltos rojos palidecen en sucesivas bellezas de recuerdo. Nombrarla es recibir de pronto el golpe de una ráfaga de viento caliente en mis mejillas frías" [NCC III 245]. Both women suffer the same fate, each a victim of an outrage. Stepens abandons Julia the night before their wedding; the narrator in "Ester Primavera" tells her a gross lie and later adds a gratuitous insult in a letter.

Arlt's finest story is without doubt "El jorobadito", a gem of perversity and paradox. The protagonist, like Stepens, is gradually enmeshed in a circumstance from which only the boldest of stratagems will extricate him. The prospective mother-in-law is more dominant than the *novia* herself, who hardly appears in the tale. But the *suegra* figure broods over the narrative and it is against her that the real battle is waged. "En la casa de la señora X yo 'hacía el novio' de una de las niñas. Es curioso. Fui atraído, insensiblemente, a la intimidad de esa familia por una hábil conducta de la señora A, que procedió con un determinado exquisito tacto y que consiste en negarnos un vaso de agua para poner a nuestro alcance, y como quien no quiere, un frasco de alcohol" [NCC III 206]. The victim is ensnared by the "hábil conducta" of the *suegra*. The other standard elements in Arlt's sex war are also present. First, the narrator's doubt whether the girl loves him as he loves her and second, his masochistic sense of inferiority. "Naturalmente, ella desde el primer día que nos tratamos me hizo experimentar con su frialdad sonriente el peso de su autoridad. Sin poder concretar en qué consistía el dominio que ejercía sobre mí, éste se traducía como la presión de una atmósfera sobre mi pasión. Frente a ella me sentía ridículo..." [NCC III 210]. Third, the false sense of purity: "De más está decir que nunca me atreví a besarla...". Trapped between mother and daughter, the coils are tightened around him. But he conceives the perverse plan of introducing the ugly hunchback, Rigoletto, into the *novia*'s family to ask for the first kiss, as proof of her love. The results are comic in the extreme. The gratuitous offence pays off but the hunchback captures the situation for himself, turning it to his own account. The originality of the theme is matched by the delicate structural balance, making it one of Arlt's most accomplished works. As to the problem we are reviewing, the result is normal: the relationship is suspended and male *lozanía* escapes intact.

Two other stories provide evidence for our hypothesis: "Tarde de domingo" and "Pequeños propietarios". The first is related to the principle of reticence, the second to the attack on marriage. Arlt was capable at times of harrowing descents into banality; "Tarde de domingo" is a product of this tendency. It recounts a meeting between Eugenio Karl (a disguised Arlt?) and a married woman, Leonilda. Karl, also married, accepts her spontaneous invitation to visit her home. She encourages his sexual advances but he finally refuses, overcome by his own pessimistic philosophy. His thinking marks an advance and a certain compassion in Arlt's ideology. Men and women are seen as victims of each other in this story, as opposed to his normal view of man as the prey. "Yo también soy un hombre bueno", says Karl. "Todos somos hombres buenos. Pero de cada uno de nosotros se burla alguna mujer, de cada mujer en alguna parte se burla un hombre. Estamos como le dije antes: a la recíproca" [NCC III 301]. Unfortunately, one has the impression of a lack of conviction in this story, reflected in technical omissions, which hobble the tale and make it too pedestrian. Arlt's best stories are built around a whimsical exaggeration or a nostalgia for lost purity, as in "Ester Primavera". The cheap domesticity of "Tarde de domingo" is its undoing.

Domesticity is also the subject of "Pequeños propietarios" but Arlt's venomous dislike of middle-class pettiness raises the artistic standard. It really belongs to that side of Arlt that produced the *Aguafuertes*, with their close scrutiny of human nature and its foibles. The result is a much enhanced vocabulary and a finer technical achievement. One of the *Aguafuertes* concerns a man –a bourgeois, of course– who steals out at night with his whole family to pilfer from a local building site. Here, the same situation is expanded into a story. Joaquin and Eufrasia suspect their neighbour of this kind of petty theft, which allows Arlt to examine their hatred of him. They pick quarrels and become involved in litigation. "El éxito de estas cuchilladas, lubricadas con jurisprudencia, no marchitaba aquel odio", he writes. What is important here is not so much the attack on bourgeois vices as the picture of their domestic contentment nurtured not on idealism but on their having a common enemy to hate. Arlt's fear of his own middle-class background and the possibility of his falling victim to its complacent embrace may readily be gathered from the closing scene:

–Mañana me averiguo dónde está la obra ...; la dirección del dueño...
–No le vas a escribir, ¡eh!
–Sí ... pero le hago un anónimo a máquina.
–¡Cómo se va a poner la hipocritona de su mujer! Fíjate que ayer con pretexto de enseñarme un figurín, me dice:
"Ah, ¿no sabe? cuando mi marido termine la obra vamos a poner persianas a todas las puertas." Y todo, ¿sabés para qué? para hacerme "estrilar".
–¡Qué gentuza!
–Y pensar que uno tiene que tratarse con ellos...
–Dejá ... mañana los arreglamos.

Bostezó Joaquin un instante, y ya cansado, dijo:
-Me voy a dormir. Hasta mañana, querida.
-¿Y no me das un beso?
-Tomá ... y que duermas bien [NCC III 275].

Prostitution and the exploitation of women

A review of the relations between the sexes in Arlt's writing would be incomplete without reference to the problem of prostitution which figures so persistently. His male characters long for purity, amidst their very anguish, yet wallow the while in their own imperfections. Erdosain's immediate response to his anguish is not to bolt into the nearest brothel for relief but to drag himself from one to the other, searching for the most vile. "Escogía con preferencia aquéllos en cuyos zaguanes veía cáscaras de naranja y regueros de ceniza...". When he plunges into his fantasies about ideal women with whom sexual contact would be impossible, his imaginings are likely to end in a conflicting desire to become a "cafishio" (another *lunfardo* term for a pimp). In stories like "Las fieras" and "Ester Primavera", not only do sexual perversities figure unashamedly but pimps and thieves abound. No doubt there is a deep-rooted desire to shock but Arlt also wishes to go further; his intentions are more serious. He seeks to demonstrate that evil and middle-class behaviour are not mutually exclusive, as we have seen in "Pequeños propietarios". Thus all his *rufianes* and *macrós* proceed from the middle class, along with the other characters. In fact, considerable emphasis –beyond that required for the normal creation of the character– is placed upon the fact that Haffner, the Rufián Melancólico, has been a teacher of mathematics. Seen from the present day, the picture that Arlt draws of Haffner's life seems to be from the depths of fantasy. In fact, it is one of the most realistic elements in the book. We have seen something of the gruesome conditions of prostitution in Buenos Aires in the 1920s. It was Arlt's self-appointed task to reveal this to the world, not out of a spirit of bravado (although he does not spare the details), but to establish how far society had gone in ensuring that reality should outstrip fantasy. Indeed, as Núñez points out, prostitution had become the career for the women who did not achieve the alternative of marriage.[29] The figures we have quoted earlier would certainly bear out this supposition.

Haffner maintains three women who bring in two thousand pesos a month. His philosophy is a debased excrescence of *machismo*, an amalgam of cynicism and sadism. "Si mañana me viniera a ver un médico", he tells Erdosain, "y me dijera: la Vasca se muere dentro de una semana la saque o no del prostíbulo, yo a la Vasca, que me ha dado treinta mil pesos en cuatro años, la dejo que trabaje los seis días y que reviente el séptimo"

[NCC I 189]. The "mujer de la vida" is the hardest and bitterest animal on earth, he contends, who complements with her masochistic attitude the sadistic exploitation of her body by her "man". "Usted cree como el noventa por ciento que el cafishio es el explotador y la prostituta la víctima. Pero dígame: ¿para qué precisa una mujer todo el dinero que gana? Lo que no han dicho los novelistas es que la mujer de la vida que no tiene hombre anda desesperada buscando uno que la engañe, que le rompa el alma de cuando en cuando y que le saque toda la plata que gana, porque es así de bestia" [NCC I 190]. Arlt neither condemns nor condones this situation, although his character Erdosain is made to express a certain shock – even he! But what Arlt seeks to demonstrate is not the parlous state of morals in the city nor even the plight of women subjected to this kind of régime; his designs are more subtle. Through his picture of prostitution, with its "respectabilities", its hierarchical structure and its codes of conduct, he is able to show that other strata of society are none the less corrupt.

> Y la gente nos cree unos monstruos, o unos animales exóticos, como nos han pintado los saineteros. Pero venga a vivir a nuestro ambiente, conózcalo, y se va a dar cuenta que es igual al de la burguesía y al de nuestra aristocracia. La mantenida desprecia a la mujer de cabaret, la mujer de cabaret deprecia a la yiranta, la yiranta desprecia a la mujer de prostíbulo y, cosa curiosa, así como la mujer que está en un prostíbulo elige casi siempre como hombre a un sujeto de avería, la de cabaret carga con un niño bien o un doctor atorrante para que la explote [NCC I 190].

So, implies the Rufián (and through him, Arlt) there is little to choose between the poses and disdain that are revealed in "Pequeños propietarios" and the same sentiments as expressed in the underworld of prostitution. Bourgeois respectability is a sham, like everything else.

That Arlt's picture of the exploitation of women is not dramatized is easily confirmed by reference to Londres's finding during exactly the same period. The parallels are astonishing at times. This is Victor, a pimp interviewed by Londres at the end of the 1920s:

> The profession of pimp, Monsieur Albert, is not so simple as that of father of a family. We must be administrators, instructors, comforters, and experts in hygiene. We need self-possession, a knowledge of character, insight, kindness, firmness and self-denial, and above all things, perseverance. ...
> As soon as they have earned twopence they do no more work. They lie in bed all day or they take lovers. They get picked up drunk, on the pavement, before they are twenty. Instead of buying underclothes they drink little glasses of white wine. They are dirty, with black nails, and uncombed hair. They soon lose all self-respect; they fight and swear. We put an end to all that. We take them and wash them and scrub them. We dress them properly and give them a taste for clean linen. And we take them away from their low companions.[30]

Compare the Rufián Melancólico discoursing to Erdosain on his "responsibilities":

> El cafishio le da a una mujer tranquilidad para ejercer su vida. Los "tiras" no la molestan. Si cae presa, él la saca; si está enferma, él la lleva a un sanatorio y la hace cuidar, y le evita líos y mil cosas fantásticas. Vea, mujer que en el ambiente trabaja por su cuenta termina siendo siempre víctima de un asalto, una estafa o un atropello bárbaro. En cambio, mujer que tiene un hombre trabaja tranquila, sosegada, nadie se mete con ella y todos la respetan [NCC I 192].

The Biblical code of the wages of sin operates, however, in Arlt's world. Haffner will not escape retribution, in spite of his self-righteous rationalizations, nor will the "fieras" in the story of that name. Haffner is shot in the back and dies in great agony but obeying the vow of silence of the underworld. He is accompanied throughout his death-throes by a member of the police department, but he refuses to name his assassin. (As Victor says to Londres, one of the rules of the Centre –presumably translated from the French "milieu"– is "to suffer the extremity of torture rather than give away a friend, even if guilty". Haffner extends this code even to his enemies.) The narrator in "La fieras" is aware that the same end awaits him. Having lost his one love –once again the loss of the ideal– he lives out his life in the same city as she, "...con la diferencia, claro está, que yo exploto a una prostituta, tengo prontuario y moriré con las espaldas desfondadas a balazos, mientras tú te casarás algún día con un empleado de banco o un subteniente de la reserva" [NCC III 277]. So, too, the underworld characters in "Ester Primavera" lie in the sanatorium with their lungs rotting.

We have tried to disentangle the ramifications of the problem of sexuality in Arlt, and in so doing we have seen that the urge to discover an ideal and pure relationship between man and woman is akin to the search for absolutes which operates throughout his creative process. Equally so, frustration of the ideal in its clash with reality may be expected to erupt in anguish. At the point where sexuality brushes against social concepts, we have discerned a dual tendency in Arlt. On the one hand, a reflection of stereotyped attitudes deriving from *machismo* and, on the other, a splenetic attack on marriage as a bourgeois institution. It is not too critical to say that Arlt's talent and originality do not lie in these areas. The attack on institutionalized sexual relations is age-old; he merely finds a niche in this worthy tradition. However, as the interpreter of the sexual *mores* of a given society at a certain time, he is invaluable. It is unlikely that he himself would have seen this as his first purpose, for he writes mainly from an indignant point of view. His outbursts, although scurrilous, are always enjoyable. They earned him the disrespect of many critics in his day. But, as Larra has said, in spite of his excesses, Arlt always remained on the side of moral honesty and human understanding.[31] Constantly vanquished in their search for the impossible, his characters never relinquish their drive towards something more noble than society can provide. They *believe* in love, as Etchenique claims:

> Como los chiquilines rabiosos que castigan a su madre rompiéndose la ropa, Arlt brama contra la mujer, la ofende, la insulta, la desprecia. Y este grito con que el hombre solitario combate al otro sexo no es más que un triste alarido de amor, una esperanzada súplica con que reclama el amor, un desesperado y último recurso con que pide el amor.[32]

CHAPTER IV

POLITICS AND SOCIETY

This is one of the most contentious areas of Arlt's writing. Since his death in 1942, his reputation as a "political" novelist has grown consistently amongst certain sections of Argentine society, largely, in our opinion, without due regard to what he actually wrote. He has been raised as a standard against bourgeois reaction by the left wing, who have claimed him amongst their ranks. He has been ignored by many intellectuals who have carped at his "bad writing". He has been read by rebellious youth for his spirit of revolt. His ambiguous relationship with Florida and Boedo suggests that by his mid-twenties he was not prepared to make a definite commitment either in artistic or political terms. By the outbreak of the Spanish Civil War, following his visit to Spain and North Africa, he was following the Communist line, according to his contemporary Juan José Gorini. [1] However, in the polarization of opinions precipitated by that war, liberal intellectuals of all kinds did likewise throughout Europe and America. The disputes about Arlt's politics, like those about his style and the influence of Dostoevsky on his work, seem to have been founded on a lack of evidence and close knowledge of what he actually wrote. One would be hard taxed to reconcile the anarchic, individualistic rebellion of his two major novels with the hard lines of left-wing thinking. Arlt's view of the world as an appearance in which reality sometimes outstrips fantasy is far removed from the deterministic theories of left-wing ideology. Gorini wrote in 1954: "Porque en realidad a él no le importaba modificar el mundo, sino descubrirlo, paladearlo. Y entenderlo. Y aun amarlo con todas sus impurezas." [2] This is too sweeping a statement, perhaps, for one can discern in Arlt more social preoccupations than it would allow. Arlt would doubtless have welcomed many social improvements but not on the political basis proposed by many of his contemporaries.

It can readily be appreciated from a reading of the novels that his political ideas and attitudes hardened during the crumbling economic situation of 1929-32. Sebreli is right to claim that his characters are, in this sense, dateable: "Pertenecen a la clase media y viven en Buenos Aires en el año 1930, no podía ser de otra manera." [3] He adds that without the economic conditions of the time, his characters' anguish would have been of a different kind. All this is very true, but it is this fact that has misled Arlt's more deterministic critics. It is the ability of Arlt's characters to assume universal stature that makes him worthy of our attention today. Writers like Castelnuovo and Mariani were also faithful representers of the social stress of the period, but they were incapable of rising to the metaphysical heights that are achieved in Arlt's fiction. Sebreli seems to be more to the point when he adds that Arlt was too preoccupied with his own relations with the world to be bothered about those in society. "En ninguno de sus libros deja traslucir que creyera en la posibilidad de una sociedad socialista."[4] Ghiano feels that Arlt disdained the puerile optimism of some writers of his generation for whom the solution lay solely in political change.[5] This is surely the real key to Arlt's position. There are moments in the Astrólogo's disquisitions on revolution and society when it is in doubt whether society's follies are under attack or those of the Astrólogo himself, such is the ambiguous cloak under which the author hides. In Arlt, as in Dostoevsky, the optimism of the revolutionary is meant to be seen as yet another part of, and not an answer to, social problems. It is therefore understandable that he should have been drawn towards the Russian's stance in *The Devils*, as more recent criticism has shown, for they both seek to reveal social ills but mock at solutions based on collective action at the expense of the individual. Even in his first novel, Silvio dreams, not of revolution or indeed social change, but of how his inventions might lift *him* out of the degradation of his social background. Erdosain and Balder have little or no sense of solidarity; they merely sneer at all those who suffer "el servilismo del cuello duro", those who squirm under a boss. There are later glimpses of solidarity in *El amor brujo*, –written during the worst effects of the depression– when Arlt criticizes young office-girls who "en vez de pensar en agremiarse para defender sus derechos, pensaban en engatusar con artes de vampiresas a un cretino adinerado que las pavoneara en una voiturette" [NCC III 61]. Even here, it is obvious from the tone that what worries him is not really the lack of union solidarity but the vampire habits of the young women. As Masotta says: "Un crítico de izquierda tendría razón de definirlo así: el hombre de Arlt, que viene de la masa, no apunta a la clase social. Esto a pesar de que su búsqueda es una empresa de *desmasificación*, en tanto quiere dejar de ser el oscuro individuo anónimo, para convertirse, en un relámpago, en sí mismo."[6] This process of "demassification", which aims to restore the individual's rights and consciousness of self, is what fundamentally distinguishes Arlt from standard centralist left-wing ideology. It would be unwise to ignore the possible influence of anarchist thought, however, which always had a strong grip in Argentina.[7] (Much of Boedo's thinking was culled from Kropotkin and Bakunin.) Communist and socialist efforts, on the other hand, are directed at the restoration of the individual's rights in a reformed social framework directed from the centre, whilst Arlt's characters are always busy opting out of any framework at all. He himself made quite clear the lack of cohesive political or social thought in his characters: "Estos individuos, canallas y tristes; viles y soñadores simultáneamente, están atados o ligados entre sí por la desesperación. La desesperación en ellos está originado, más que por la pobreza material, por otro factor: la desorientación que, después de la gran guerra, ha revolucionado la conciencia de los hombres, dejándolos vacíos de ideales y esperanzas. Hombres y mujeres en la novela [*Los siete locos*] rechazan el presente y la civilización, tal cual está organizada. Quisieran creer en algo, arrodillarse ante algo, amar algo..." And he adds: "...la angustia de estos hombres nace de su esterilidad interior".[8] The key to our understanding of his political attitude lies in that telling phrase "Quisieran creer en algo" and it is to this end that the Astrólogo's imaginings set about offering a spurious solution.

Arlt was obviously aware of the broad lines of left-wing ideology. The hotchpotch of political thought advanced by his characters shows a general, if unsophisticated knowledge. He had lived through a period of acute change during which the theories of Bolshevism were speading round the world, following the 1917 Revolution. We may assume that he had heard endless debate and argument during his adolescence and early manhood. Nevertheless, a reading of his works would not allow any specific conclusions as to his allegiances. Etchenique claims that he was bad material for any political party with his "individualismo feroz, despótico y arbitrario."[9] Knowing his sombre view of human kind, it is time to see the proposals in his fiction for what they are: an extended irony aimed at simplistic revolutionary ideology. Too little has been made of the distinction between sincere social comment and ironic, black humour. The revolutionary "proposals", in our view, belong to the latter, whilst the compassionate observation of human beings and society in parts of the novels and many of the *Aguafuertes* belong squarely to the former. Like many of his contemporaries, under the pressure of the new existential thinking of his time, Arlt believed that the real revolution was to be achieved in the individual and not in the mass.

Admittedly, as his writing progresses, there is a noticeable shift from fantastic reactions to social inequality and injustice towards more concrete social observation. At the beginning of *Los siete locos*, as in its predecessor, the protagonist dreams of solutions to his oppressed condition which are engendered in his fantasy. As he wanders through the wealthier areas of the city, his reaction to the splendour he comes across is not one of rejection or revolt; he merely wonders how quickly he can join it. "Aquél era otro mundo dentro de la ciudad canalla que él conocía, otro mundo para el que su corazón latía con palpitaciones lentas y pesadas" [NCC I 176]. As the novel advances, more serious social comment makes its intrusion. The Astrólogo becomes Arlt's mouthpiece not only for harebrained revolutionary schemes but also for soundly-based strictures on society. He proposes a revolution centred on a great lie, with an electric chair on every street corner, or a guillotine from which the heads will roll like grapes at harvest-time, innocent and guilty alike, to satisfy the people's craving for sensation. To this satire of degraded human nature belong his ideas for financing the revolution by a chain of brothels (perhaps not so outlandish if one bears in mind the horrifying facts and figures) and the search for some symbol to inflame the plebs: "...¿Sabe ahora lo que nos hace falta? Es descubrir un símbolo vulgar para entusiasmar al populacho... Hay que descubrir algo grosero y estúpido ... algo que entre por los sentidos de la multitud como la camisa negra... Ese diablo [Mussolini] ha tenido talento. Descubrió que la psicología del pueblo italiano era una psicología de barbero y tenor de opereta..." It is not only the thoughtless populace that comes in for such treatment. When the revolutionaries assemble, the Mayor (a spurious Major who turns out to be real after all) seizes the opportunity to spread the criticism to the Cámara de Diputados, accusing them of being sold to foreign companies, whilst the Communists, too, receive their share of lambasting, being qualified as "un bloque de carpin-teros que desbarran sobre sociología en una cuadra". The whole thing is a romp with Arlt enjoying himself mightily. However, by the time he composes *Los lanzallamas*, following the conservative *pronunciamiento* of 1930, the satirical and bantering tone gives way to harder reactions. Capitalist society, in complicity with atheism, has turned man into a sceptical monster, "verdugo de sus semejantes por el placer de un cigarro, de una comida o de un vaso de vino. Cobarde, astuto, mezquino, lascivo, escéptico, avaro y glotón, del hombre actual no debemos esperar nada" [NCC II 28]. And yet, the Astrólogo's ideas for the promotion of the revolution change not one whit throughout the two volumes: the great "mentira metafísica" which will satisfy man's hunger for belief. But comments on society become more astringent and more pertinent. His philosophy is an amalgam of megalomania (which would like to shake the world by the ears) and sensible social criticism. His lunacy, which would put to death those who constitute a danger to the revolutionary cause –and many who do not– provides Arlt with a splendid cover for his anarchistic attack on society. If we were to sum up this aspect of Arlt's thinking, we might say that his social strictures are always valid, or at least meant to be taken seriously, whilst the political solutions put forward belong to his world of fantasy, in which death-rays, phosgene factories, guillotines and electric chairs abound. He slips quick-footedly from one to the other; woe betide the reader who fails to notice the change in step. It was his inability to control this process that finally aborted *Los lanzallamas*. Death-rays and poisonous gases overwhelm the social awareness; destructive adolescent fantasies take over. Too much attention is given to daydreams towards the end of the work and too little to the sharp-edged satire in which he excelled.

Returning to Dostoevsky, we may now establish certain further textual parallels. In *The Devils*[10] Verkhovensky's "group of five" assembles at Virginsky's house. "The five chosen ones were sitting now at the general table and very skilfully assumed the air of ordinary men, so that no one would notice them."[11] (A noteworthy detail; with Verkhovensky's group, but not part of it, is an army major. Arlt, too, includes the Major amongst his *seven* conspirators.[12] Haffner, looking ordinary like Dostoevsky's revolutionaries, "está leyendo unos papeles en blanco"!) The dynamic for the Russian group consists in the murder of Shatov by the rest, an idea first proposed by Stavrogin. Similarly, Erdosain proposes the murder of Barsut to the Astrólogo, who readily accepts the plan. The motive is different, however; Shatov is to be killed in order to bind the conspirators together in secrecy, whilst Barsut is to be sacrificed ostensibly for his money. Shatov is in fact killed; in Arlt's novel, the Astrólogo deliberately contrives a mock murder, deceiving Erdosain and producing one of the most hilarious black scenes in Arlt's writing. So much for the general framework.

The ravings of the Astrólogo derive directly from those of Verkhovensky, in their combination of millenarian belief and political cynicism. The Russian proposes to use the aristocratic Stavrogin as a figurehead for the cause; he will be wheeled on to the stage to satisfy the mob's need to identify with some eminent personage. The Astrólogo proposes a figurehead like Krishnamurti, taken from Theosophy, some boy-god who will dazzle the multitudes. "We shall say he is in hiding", Verkhovensky said quietly, in a sort of amorous whisper, as though he were really drunk. "Do you know what the expression in hiding means? But he will appear. He will appear. We shall spread a legend which will be much better than that of the sect of castrates. He exists, but no one has ever seen him. Oh, what a wonderful legend one could spread! And the main thing is – a new force is coming. And that's what they want. That's what they're weeping for."[13] This cynicism finds its reflection in the Astrólogo's boy-god. "Para la comedia del dios eligiremos un adolescente ... Mejor será criar un niño de excepcional belleza, y se le educará para hacer el papel de dios. Hablaremos ... se hablará de él por todas partes, pero con misterio, y la imaginación de la gente multiplicará su prestigio" [NCC I 272]. Arlt's adaptation seems obvious. "You see, I'm a rogue, and not a socialist" cries Verkhovensy. "Yo lo creía a usted obrerista", says the Abogado to the Astrólogo. "Cuando converse con un proletario seré rojo", he replies. "Ahora converso con usted. ... Seremos bolcheviques, católicos, fascistas, ateos, militaristas, en diversos grados de iniciación" [NCC I 273]. The Astrólogo proposes *autos de fe* in the streets to inspire the latent madmen in society. So, too, Verkhovensky relies on the hidden resentment and irrationality of the populace. Schoolboys who kill a peasant for the sake of a thrill will swell their ranks; juries who acquit criminals without distinction, administrators, authors, – "oh, there are lots and lots of us, and they don't know it themselves", he cries. Examples of this kind might be multiplied, but the foregoing will certainly show that Arlt dipped more than carelessly into Dostoevsky's novel. Nor would it be exaggerating a point to see in Stavrogin's perverse marriage to the *crippled* Miss Lebyatkin a parallel with Ergueta's marriage to Hipólita, whom he insists on calling "la Coja". There is also a fundamental theme running through both works: that of man's aspirations to become God. In *The Devils*, Kirilov's argument leads to the belief that through suicide he himself will become God. The only real aspiration for man, the Astrólogo tells Barsut, is to wish to become God, "querer ser Dios, confundirse con Dios". Dostoevsky not only worked out his own religious problems through his novels but he reconstituted this exercise in exciting narrative. Arlt could not be accused of novelizing his religious feelings, but the ravings of characters like Ergueta, the religious fanatic, in conversation with Barsut, are wholly reminiscent of the Russian's lengthy dialogues on religion. We do not mean to belittle Arlt by these references to Dostoevsky, nor to detract from the power of his characters. They are not transplants from Russian literature by any means. They are indigenous creations growing out of Arlt's experience of people he met in Buenos Aires, as he himself maintains. "Son individuos y mujeres de esta ciudad a quienes yo he conocido."[14] But it is pointless to deny, as some have done, that these affinities and influences exist. No literature grows out of the void; it sinks its roots in what has gone before. If it did not, it would be the worse for that.

Arlt's "revolution" is, then, a protest, a cry against the dehumanizing forces in the society of his day, a cry against not only the governing classes but against the proletarian hordes who condone their influence.

> Viven. Eso. Mecanizados como hormigas. Con un itinerario permanente. Casa, oficina, oficina, casa. Café. Del café al prostíbulo. Del prostíbulo al cine. Itinerario permanente. Gestos permanentes. Pensamientos. Cumplimos nuestros deberes. ¡Somos honestos! Somos vírgenes [NCC III 98].

His exhortation is to personal rebellion, not to planned revolution. In his novels the real battle is joined in the individual; in an Erdosain grappling with his anguish or a Balder with his disgust or a Hipólita with her poverty – all struggling to escape from the "rebaño de esclavos que agonizan en la ciudad". The solution to these creatures' anguish does not lie in collectivity; there is nothing in Arlt to suggest such an outcome. It is towards individualization that he aims. The solution is personal and existential.

> –¿Qué me importa a mí la felicidad de los otros? Yo quiero mi felicidad. Mi

felicidad. Yo, Yo, Hipólita. Con mi cuerpo, que tiene tres pecas, una bajo el brazo, otra en la espalda, otra bajo el seno derecho [NCC II 95].

"¿Cómo se busca la verdad?" asks Barsut of the Astrólogo. "Buscándose a sí mismo", is the reply. "La verdad es el Hombre. El Hombre con su cuerpo" [NCC II 70 and 21]. Under no circumstances can Arlt's solutions for the ills he recognizes around him be interpreted as socialistic. There are times when they are anarchistic, even nihilist, with the total destruction of society as an immediate goal. But Kropotkin, one of the theoretical fathers of Argentine anarchism, never advocated the attack on mechanized society which is a kingpin of Arlt's ideology.[15] The latter's view of technological society as destructive of individuality belongs foursquare to the contemporary polemic against scientism, to the existential revolution of the day. A character like Erdosain, who "reconocía que tenía el espíritu sucio de asco a la vida" was not to be cured by utopian collectivism. Arlt sought to make the individual aware, not to reform him.

The Aguafuertes

If one reads only Arlt's novels, with their undiluted pessimism and lack of constructive solutions, one would take away a sombre picture indeed. They are not even redeemed by their humour in the final analysis, for this, too, is black in the extreme. Fortunately, they are not the whole Arlt by any means. We have been concerned so far with his ideology and have perforce stayed within the realm of his fictional prose. But he lived by the pen, as so many Argentine writers have done, not only as a reporter but as an *aguafuertista*. It is to his *Aguafuertes porteñas* that we turn finally, for, although they carry no specific ideology, they offer a social documentation of the Buenos Aires of the 1930s in which their author's love of humanity and his compassion for its distress and follies is never far below the surface. They provide a valuable and often humorous antidote to the grey tones of the novels and will allow us to put a gloss on some of the ideas that have emerged so far. Pedro Orgambide said of this aspect of his work: "Arlt, en la crónica, es el equivalente de un Daumier. Sus apuntes son uno de los testimonios más fieles de un tiempo de crisis y definición. Y, lo mismo que un Daumier, la risa se enciende entre los laberintos de un tiempo en que la risa es desterrada. Es su 'cura de salud'."[16] Since their original publication in the 1930s there have been three editions in book form in 1950, 1960 and 1969 and, subsequently, a series of re-editions during the 1970s, a fact which is testimony to their continuing popularity and relevance. Arlt wrote them from day to day in an haphazard fashion but later editions have sought to impose some order by re-classifying them into, for example, articles on women, *porteño* types, the social crisis. This zeal for order was never very apparent in their author, who worked as the inspiration moved him, now prompted by some picturesque *lunfardismo*, as in "Divertido origen de la palabra 'squenum' ", or some colloquialism as in "Apuntes filosóficos acerca del 'hombre que se tira a muerto' ", now pinning down a whole social class by an apparently insignificant detail. To classify the *Aguafuertes* is to detract from their spontaneity. A number of articles collected together on the theme, say, of *porteña* womanhood and their charms and vices is to assume a continuity of thought that Arlt never enjoyed. Whilst we have chosen to classify his ideas, perhaps arbitrarily at times, it seems inadvisable to impose such a straitjacket on these delightful cameos of Buenos Aires life. An important feature is their use of *lunfardo*, an important component of his style. It is fair to conclude that, whilst his call in his political ideas is to individual rebellion, in the *Aguafuertes* his linguistic technique relies largely for its appeal on class solidarity, often summed up in one or two typical *lunfardo* terms which act as "in-group" indicators. This aspect of his writing rightly belongs to an examination of his technique, but without being aware of his methods, we should fail to appreciate some of the more enjoyable elements in these articles. In the following passage, quoted at some length, the trivial detail of the chair placed outside the house to enjoy the evening air, so common in Latin countries at dusk, is used to reveal a whole substratum of Buenos Aires society. Unashamedly nostalgic in tone, it relies entirely on the esoteric slang of *lunfardo* to provide the reader with a sense of belonging. It does not succumb to the dangers of dialect writing, in which the local terminology becomes more important than the content. As Pagés Larraya says, the secret of the great popularity of the *Aguafuertes* lies in their "sutil identificación de tema y estilo".[17]

> Llegaron las noches de las sillas en la vereda: de las familias estancadas en las puertas de sus casas; llegaron las noches del amor sentimental, del "buenas noches, vecina", el político e insinuante "¿cómo le va don Pascual?" Y don Pascual sonríe y se atusa los "baffi", que bien sabe por qué el mocito le pregunta cómo va. Llegaron las noches...
>
> Yo no sé qué tienen estos barrios porteños tan tristes en el día bajo el sol, y tan lindos cuando la luna los recorre oblicuamente. Yo no sé qué tienen; que reos o inteligentes, vagos o activos, todos queremos este barrio con su jardín (sitio para la futura sala) y sus pebetas siempre iguales y siempre distintas, y sus viejos, siempre iguales y siempre distintos, también.
>
> Encanto mafioso, dulzura mistonga, ilusión baratieri, ¿qué sé yo qué tienen todos estos barrios? estos barrios porteños, largos, todos cortados con la misma tijera, todos semejantes con sus casitas atorrantas, sus jardines con la palmera al centro y unos yuyos semiflorecidos que aroman como si la noche reventara por ellos el apasionamiento que encierran las almas de la ciudad; almas que sólo saben el ritmo del tango y del "te quiero". Fulería poética, eso y algo más [AP 79].

It would be difficult to believe that this was the same Buenos Aires as that of the novels, with their geometric planes and stark contrast of light and dark, "esta puerca ciudad", as he calls it now and then. In the novels, man and his environment are at odds and the anguish of one and the other interpenetrates. In the *Aguafuertes*, the city and its dwellers are at one, in harmony. Not that life is ever depicted as easy; the time is 1930 and the depression is upon us. But the bitterness of the fictional works is absent here, a gentle irony replacing the spleen. One can imagine the sense of solidarity, a solidarity born of adversity, that a reader of *El Mundo* (where many of these articles were first published) might have experienced on coming across the following:

> Y he pensado en el hombre del umbral; he pensado en la dulzura de estar sentado en mangas de camiseta en el mármol de una puerta. En la felicidad de estar casado con una planchadora y decirle:
> –Nena; dame quince guitas para un paquete de cigarillos.
> Han venido días tibios. No sé si se han fijado en el fenómeno; pero todos aquéllos que tienen un pantalón calafateado, emparchado o taponado, que según las averías del traje se puede definir el género de costura, remiendo, parche o zurcido; todos aquéllos que tienen un traje averiado sobre las asentaderas, meditan con semblante compungido en la brevedad del imperio del sobretodo. Porque no se puede negar: el sobretodo, por rasposo que sea, presta un servicio. Es cómplice y cubridor. Encubre la roña de abajo, las roturas del lienzo. Si siempre hiciera frío, la gente podría prescindir de los sastres y hacerse un traje cada cinco años [AP 157].

Figures from the novels appear here and there, like the prospective *suegra* who dispatches the younger son to keep an eye on the doings of her daughter and the *novio*; the child must be bought off by frequent greasing of the palm. But normally the gallery of *porteño* types exists in its own right, like the *curanderas* who are "unas furbas de más de treinta años. Gastan lutos y en la garganta una cinta de terciopelo negro, que agrisa el polvo de arroz y la natural grasitud de sus pescuezos de gallina" [NAP 279]. Arlt had a Quevedo-like eye for the detail with which to transfix a whole character and, as with Quevedo, realism often spills over into the grotesque. Perhaps this was essential to his success. Note how the simile used to describe the cat's tail in the following sequence is wholly fantastic and is introduced, not so much to support the description, as to add a touch of the grotesque which will round off the paragraph. Once again he is describing the *curanderas*:

> Reciben a determinada hora, y siempre son viudas. Cuando hablan del esposo dicen: "Que en paz descanse el bendito". Conocen más nombres de santos que el mismísimo martirologio y más milagros que los propios bolandistas. Hablan del ectoplasma y del periespíritu. Hacen confidencias de revelaciones, y tienen un gato negro con una cola que parece alambre de púa [NAP 279].

The simile does not support the fact; the fact is introduced to allow the simile. Such descriptions are, more often than not, spiced with social comment proffered in a bantering fashion. The *curandera* is not merely picturesque; she is a swindler, but likeable withall. So too with the whole stream of characters and types who pass through these articles. Arlt puts his readers on their guard but finally turns a blind eye to such human failings, as in his description of the *furbo* (swindler):

> En nuestra ciudad se reconoce como típico ejemplar del "furbo", el rematador por ocasiones, el corredor de ventas de casa a mensualidades, el comerciante que siempre falla, y arregla el "asunto" en el "concordato". Típicamente está encuadrado dentro del orden comercial, sus astucias engañadoras se magnifican y ejercitan dentro del terreno de los negocios. Así el "furbo" venderá una casa asentada en barro y construída con pésimos materiales, por "buena"; si es rematador, sólo intervendrá en tratos equívocos; si es comerciante, desaparecerá un día, dejando una enorme cantidad de deudas pequeñas que suman una grande, pero que en resumen no alcanzan individualmente la importancia necesaria para hacerlo procesar, y por donde vaya, entre amigos y enemigos, entre conocidos y desconocidos, hará alguna de las "suyas", sin que la gente alcance a irritarse al grado de tratar de romperle el alma, porque en medio de todo reconocerá sonriendo que es un "furbo". Y qué se le va a hacer... [AP 47].

So the Turkish carpet-seller, the woman who overspends on the *quinielas*, the bachelor, the liar, the persistent malingerer, the peeping Tom who spies into houses from his flat roof, and a hundred others, are all the subject of well-aimed but indulgent censure. The only figure for whom there is no compassion, as in the novels, is the bourgeois. Arlt's bitterness is consistently turned against the small property owner and shopkeeper in his fiction, as we have seen, because in their greed they have "taken their eyes off the stars". But in the *Aguafuertes* the loathing is muted. Nowhere does one find the nauseous reaction of Erdosain against "los tenderos que desde el fondo de sus covachas escupían a la oblicuidad de la lluvia". His gall is now tempered by understanding, as in his depiction of the café owner who is torn between saving eighty pesos a month by having his comely wife attend to the phonograph and his jealousy at the avid eyes cast over her anatomy by his clients [AP 67]. In all these cases, Arlt's regard for his fellow-man, even in the most ridiculous plight as with the café owner, is paramount and assuages the rancour that invests the fictional works. The *Aguafuertes* –human, subjective and ironic– are an equally valid attempt to come to terms with the realities of the great city as are the novels. They display a compassionate facet of their author's temperament that the novels would never suggest. These qualities are acutely seen in "Atenti, nena, que el tiempo pasa", in which Arlt takes the *carpe diem* theme and makes it his own, couching it in thoroughly *porteño* terms. The irony and grotesque exaggeration would not be out of place in Quevedo. Arlt has seen a young woman on the tram playing haughty to her unprepossessing boyfriend. His hatred of sham and conceit leads to a piece of compelling popular philosophy. It is necessary to quote at some length to savour the atmosphere and the rich slang.

> No lo desprecies al tipo que llevás al lado. No, nena: no lo desprecies.
> El tiempo, esa abstracción matemática que revuelve la sesera a todos los otarios con patentes de sabios existe, nena. Existe para escarnio de tu trompita que dentro del algunos años tendrá más arrugas que guante de vieja o traje de cesante.
> ¡Atenti, piba, que los siglos corren!
> Cierto es que tu novio tiene cara de zanahoria, con nariz fuera de ordenanza y los "tegobitos" como los de una foca. Cierto que en cada fosa nasal puede llevar contrabando, y que tiene la mirada pitañosa como sirviente sin sueldo o babión sin destino, cierto que hay muchachos más lindos, más simpáticos, más ranas, más prácticos para pulsar la vihuela de tu corazón y cualquier cosa que se le ocurra al que me lee. Cierto es. Pero el tiempo pasa, a pesar de que Spencer decía que no existía, y Einstein afirme que es una realidad de la geometría euclidiana que no tiene minga que ver con las otras geometrías... ¡Atenti, nena, que el tiempo pasa! Pasa. Y cada día merma el stock de giles. Cada día desaparece un zonzo de la circulación. Parece mentira, pero así no más es.
> Te advierto el pensmiento, percalera. Es éste: "Puede venir otro mejor..."
> Cierto ... Pero pensá que todos quieren tomarle tacto a la mercadería, pulsar la estofa, saber lo que compran, para batir después que no les gusta, y ¡qué diablo! Recordate que ni en las ferias se permite tocar la manteca, que la ordenanza municipal en los puestos de los turcos bien claro lo dice: "Se prohibe tocar la carne", pero que esas ordenanzas en la caza del novio, en el clásico del civil, no rezan, y que muchas veces hay que infringir el digesto municipal para llegar al registro nacional.
> ¿Que el hombre es feo como un gorila? Cierto es; pero si te acostumbras a mirarlo te va a parecer más lindo que Valentino. Después que un novio no vale por la cara, sino por otras cosas. Por el sueldo, por lo empacador de vento que sea, por lo cuidadoso del laburo ... por los ascensos que puede tener ... en fin ... por muchas cosas. Y el tiempo pasa, nena. Pasa al galope; pasa con bronca. Y cada día merma el stock de los zanahorias; cada día desaparece de la circulación un zonzo. Algunos que se mueren, otros que se avivan... [AP 116].

This amalgam of gentle censure and compassionate observation, allied to the deft handling of *lunfardo* and other slang terms,[18] reveals a very different Arlt from that of the fictional works. Where the novels and the *Aguafuertes* find common ground is in their moral stand against all who satisfy their own desires at the expense of others, those who damage illusions and destroy the gentleness of life. For, in spite of his caustic remarks and hatred of so much that society had created around him in an implacable city, his was a gentle and receptive soul. As one of his characters says: "Yo te amo, vida, a pesar de todo lo que te afearon los hombres".

NOTES

INTRODUCTION

1. R. Larra, *Roberto Arlt el torturado* (Buenos Aires, 1950). References to this work relate to the second edition of 1956. All books or reviews quoted are published in Buenos Aires unless otherwise stated.
2. N. Etchenique, *Roberto Arlt* (1962).
3. See *Conducta*, no. 21 (Jul.-Aug. 1942).
4. See *Contorno*, no. 2 (May 1954).
5. S. Goštautas, *Buenos Aires y Arlt* (Madrid, 1977).
6. A. Núñez, *La obra narrativa de Roberto Arlt* (1968).
7. O. Masotta, *Sexo y traición en Roberto Arlt* (1965).
8. D. Maldavsky, *Las crisis en la narrativa de Roberto Arlt* (1968). See also D. Guerrero, *Roberto Arlt, el habitante solitario* (1972).
9. A. W. Hayes, *Roberto Arlt: la estrategia de su ficción* (London, 1981). See also B. Pastor, *Roberto Arlt y la rebelión alienada* (Gaithersburg, 1980) which reverts to a more socially-based interpretation.
10. C. Mastronardi, *Formas de la realidad nacional* (1961), 109.
11. See the prologue to the second edition of *El juguete rabioso* (1950).
12. R. Castagnino, *El teatro de Roberto Arlt* (La Plata, 1964), 14.
13. G. Ara, *Los argentinos y la literatura nacional* (1966), 119.
14. See A. Chapman, "Manuel Gálvez y Eduardo Mallea", *Revista Iberoamericana* (Pittsburgh, Oct. 1953) Vol. XIX, no. 37, 71-78.
15. J. Mafud, *El desarraigo argentino* (1959), 98.
16. The population of Argentina grew from 3,954,900 (1895 census) to 7,884,900 (1914 census), during the period that immediately precedes Arlt's entry into the novel. Almost 6,000,000 of the 1914 population lived on the *litoral*. See J. L. Romero, *El desarrollo de las ideas en la sociedad argentina del siglo veinte* (Mexico, 1965).
17. The effects of immigration and industrialization on Argentine literature have been studied by Maldavsky, *Las crisis*, pp. 103 ff. See also Gladys N. Onega, *La inmigración en la literatura argentina* (Univ. Nac. del Litoral, 1965).
18. T. Carella, *Picaresca porteña* (1966), 28.
19. The following figures for strikes in Argentina are revealing in this connection. 1917: 138; 1918: 196; 1919: 367. (See Romero, *El desarrollo* p. 87). The brutality with which the strikes were put down

finally in 1919 led to the incorporation into Argentine social history of the famous expression "la semana trágica".

20. M. S. Stabb, *In Quest of Identity* (Chapel Hill, 1967), 5.
21. Romero, *El desarrollo*, 85.
22. We shall use the following notation throughout this study for reference to works by Arlt: NCC: *Novelas completas y cuentos* (Fabril Editora, 1963), Volumes I, II and III. AP: *Aguafuertes porteñas* (Editorial Futuro, 1950). NAP: *Nuevas aguafuertes porteñas* (Librería Hachette, 1960). Other works will be referred to in full.
23. J. Franco, *An Introduction to Spanish-American Literature* (Cambridge, 1969), 80.
24. Mafud, *El desarraigo*, 103.
25. See, for example, Margaret Wood, *Paths of Loneliness* (New York, 1953).
26. R. Scalabrini Ortiz, *El hombre que está solo y espera* (1931). References are to the 7th. edition (1941).
27. Scalabrini, *El hombre*, 45.
28. Scalabrini, *El hombre*, 65.
29. Scalabrini, *El hombre*, 65.
30. H. Murena, *El pecado original de América* (1965).
31. Murena, *El pecado*, 71.
32. A. Prieto, *Estudios de literatura argentina* (1969), 60.
33. Goštautas, *Buenos Aires*, 184.
34. Etchenique, *Roberto Arlt*, 29.
35. Larra, *Roberto Arlt*, 56.
36. L. Harss, *Los nuestros* (1968), 253.

CHAPTER I

1. R. Mariani, "Roberto Arlt", *Conducta*, no. 21, Jul.-Aug. 1942.
2. Masotta seems to come across this difficulty. He says: "Arlt es uno de esos escritores que hablan abundantemente para negarse a hablar clara y expresamente". *Sexo*, 39.
3. "Roberto Arlt sostiene que es de los escritores que van a quedar y hace una inexorable crítica sobre la poca consistencia de la obra de los otros" *La literatura argentina* (Aug. 1929, núm. aniversario), 25-27.
4. L. Barletta, *Boedo y Florida: una versión distinta* (1967), 48.
5. Arlt, *La literatura*, 26. (My italics.)
6. Larra, *Roberto Arlt*, 80.
7. Goštautas, *Buenos Aires*, 49.
8. A. Yunque, *Literatura social en la Argentina* (1941), 324.
9. "Florida de arrabal" by Dante A. Linyera (pseudonym of F. B. Rimoli).

10. The Boedo group also published other reviews like *Dínamo, Extrema Izquierda, Acción de Arte, Suplemento de la Protesta,* whilst Florida produced *Inicial, Proa* "y alborotaron los sótanos del viejo Royal Keller con la tumultuosa *Revista Oral*" as Yunque says.

11. D. Cúneo, *Aventura y letra de América Latina* (1964), 19.

12. A. Prieto, *Estudios de literatura argentina* (1969), 52. For more detailed study of the Florida/Boedo dispute, see also Larra, pp. 65 ff; J. L. Romero, pp. 125 ff; G. de Torre, *Historia de las literaturas de vanguardia* (Madrid, 1965), 584; Goštautas, pp. 36 ff. and Barletta, *Boedo.*

13. It is surely wrong to suggest, as Jean Franco does, that Arlt was at a loss as to how to end the book. This is, on the contrary, one of the originalities of the work. See J. Franco, *Introduction,* 303.

14. Gide published his study of Dostoevsky in 1923.

15. "Mito y realidad de Roberto Arlt", *Ficción,* no. 17, 1959, 96-100.

16. Goštautas, *Buenos Aires,* 98 ff..

17. Mastronardi, *Formas,* 114.

18. Comparisons with Mallea are particularly appropriate. Arlt was born in 1900, Mallea in 1903. The concept in question lies at the heart of Mallea's *Simbad,* in which his protagonist Fernando says: "Si me hubiera visto tantas noches despierto, pensando en seres que no conozco, que sé que viven en alguna parte con dolores que comparto, con las vicisitudes que compadezco, con los conflictos que me gustaría ayudarles a resolver". *Simbad* (1957), 356. "He sufrido por mí, y por los otros, ¿se da cuenta? también por los otros..." cries Erdosain [NCC I 247].

19. D. Cúneo, *Aventura,* 188.

20. M. Molinari, "Roberto Arlt", *Contorno,* no. 2 (May 1954), 9.

21. Mallea writes of "...toda la hostilidad cruel de la ciudad recogida en su deliberado e indestructible mutismo" (*Historia de una pasión argentina*).

22. Núñez, *La obra narrativa,* 88.

23. Upton Sinclair, *The Jungle* (London, 1936), 214. First published in 1906.

24. Mafud, *El desarraigo,* 98.

25. N. Jitrik, *Escritores argentinos: dependencia o libertad* (1967). J. L. Romero calls 1926 "un año de revelaciones de la nueva sensibilidad, del espíritu nuevo", *El desarrollo,* 122.

26. Arlt achieves stylistic effects by a constant transposition of epithets. A further linguistic detail is that both he and Céline use the rare term *relentes* and *relents* to suggest the vapours and smells.

27. L. F. Céline, *Voyage au bout de la nuit* (Paris, 1952), 241.

28. Céline, *Voyage,* 225.

29. Paradoxically, Arlt remained a confirmed city dweller throughout his short life. As Larra says, his only contact with the countryside, during his brief stay in Córdoba, was a very negative experience for him.
30. Etchenique, *Roberto Arlt*, 13.
31. Etchenique, *Roberto Arlt*, 48.
32. Masotta, *Sexo*, 27.
33. See J. M. Flint, "Rasgos comunes en algunos de los personajes de Eduardo Mallea", *Iberoromania* (Munich, Dec. 1969), no. 4, 340-45.
34. Ulíses Petit de Murat writes of Arlt: "Creador nato, sus invenciones se mantienen exclusivamente a sus expensas" *Síntesis*, Año IV, Oct. 1930, no. 41, 161. Juan José Sebreli, in the only article published on Arlt in Victoria Ocampo's *Sur*, makes the same point, stating that all his characters are part of himself. "Inocencia y culpabilidad de Roberto Arlt", *Sur*, no. 223, (1953), 109-19.
35. Masotta, *Sexo*, 99.
36. See Maldavsky, *Las crisis*, 64.
37. Larra, *Roberto Arlt*, 23.
38. It may not be coincidental that Dostoievski's father was equally domineering and cruel.

CHAPTER II

1. Parts of this chapter and Chapter IV have been reworked from articles published in *Iberoamerikanisches Archiv*. I am grateful to the Editor for his permission to do so.
2. See J. M. Flint, "Politics and Society in the novels of Roberto Arlt", *Iberoamerikanisches Archiv*, II, no. 2, 155 ff. Goštautas *Buenos Aires*, pp. 98 ff., also devotes considerable attention to this matter.
3. A. Gide, *Dostoevsky* (Eng. translation, Harmondsworth, 1967), 83.
4. Gide, *Dostoevsky*, 86.
5. See E. Fromm, *The Art of Loving* (New York, 1956).
6. Goštautas, *Buenos Aires*, 98 ff. examines *Notes from Underground* at some length and Arlt's relations to it.
7. F. Dostoevsky, *Notes from Underground* (New York, 1961), 94.
8. Dostoevsky, *Notes*, 118.
9. Dostoevsky, *Notes*, 201.
10. It is of note that Stavrogin, in *The Devils*, proposes to "...commit some crime, I mean, something shameful, something really disgraceful, something very mean and ridiculous, so that people would remember it *for a thousand years*." (my italics).
11. Others shroud their opinions in vague phrases. "Es algo así como el Dostoiewski de la generación del '22", J. Pinto, *Breviario de literatura argentina contemporánea* (1958), 111.

12. Larra, *Roberto Arlt*, 52.
13. Murena, *El pecado*, 93 (my italics).
14. M. Arlt, Introduction to *Novelas Completas y Cuentos*, 20. In her subsequent introduction to the paperback edition of her father's novels, she significantly omits any reference to Tolstoi.
15. In a round table discussion on the state of Argentine literature –"¿Existe una nueva literatura?"– tape-recorded and published in *Primera Plana* (date unknown). In the same discussion, Roger Pla refers to *Los siete locos* as "la primera novela experimental argentina".
16. Goštautas, *Buenos Aires*, 98.
17. In the article "Roberto Arlt sostiene..." (*La literatura argentina*, 26). Arlt said in 1929 that of the works recently published in Buenos Aires the following would survive the years: Güiraldes's *Don Segundo Sombra*, Castelnuovo's *Tinieblas*, Mallea's *Cuentos para una inglesa desesperada* and his own *El juguete rabioso*.
18. Even Mallea's famous dichotomy of "la Argentina visible" and "invisible" is to be found in Scalabrini in 1931.
19. Masotta, *Sexo*, 31.
20. Stabb, *In Quest*, 169.
21. See Flint, "Rasgos comunes en algunos de los personajes de Eduardo Mallea", *Iberoromania* (Munich, Dec. 1969), no. 4, 340-45.

CHAPTER III

1. Maldavsky's study of this aspect of Arlt's work is unbalanced, based as it is on his theory of a strong Oedipus complex in Arlt. It takes little account of existing social or collective ideas.
2. Nalé Roxlo, in his book on Alfonsina Stornis, points out that she was the first woman to sit at table at a literary luncheon in Buenos Aires. Hitherto, the women had customarily sat in the balcony to watch the men eat! He also adds the telling detail that when the *colectivos* were first introduced in 1928, women were forbidden to ride in them. *Genio y figura de Alfonsina Storni* (1964), 14.
3. H. E. Lewald, *Buenos Aires: retrato de una sociedad hispánica a través de su literatura* (Boston, 1968), 42.
4. Scalabrini, *El hombre*, 42.
5. Scalabrini, *El hombre*, 42.
6. Albert Londres, a French journalist, gives a vivid account of the trade in women between French ports and Buenos Aires in *The Road to Buenos Ayres* (London, 1928). We shall have occasion to refer to his work later.
7. T. Carella, *Picaresca porteña* (1966), 10.
8. Londres, *The Road*, 93. Arlt's figures in *Los siete locos* are very close. But he also adds bribes to the police, doctors' fees, etc.

9. Londres, *The Road*, 125.
10. Carella, *Picaresca*, 28.
11. From the French *maquereau*, argot for pimp. This term and *canfinflero* are common *lunfardo* coinage.
12. A. Jauretche, *El medio pelo en la sociedad argentina* (1967), 182.
13. Examples of tangos are taken from J. Gobello and E. Stilman, *Las letras del tango de Villoldo a Borges* (1965) and from I. Vilariño, *Las letras de tango* (1965). Arlt makes only one reference to the tango, in "Ester Primavera", where the inmates in the sanitorium sing and play one [NCC III 245].
14. Mafud, *El desarraigo*, 102.
15. In the excellent edition of *Los caprichos* by Dover Publications (New York, 1969) see, for example, "La filiación", which bears the caption: "Aqui se trata de engatusar al novio haciendole ver pr. la egecuta. quienes fueron los padres, abuelos, visabuelos y tatarabs. de la Srta. y ella quien es? luego la verá." Or "Todos caerán", in which women, old and young, are seen stripping young cocks of their feathers and cleaning them out like chickens ready for the oven. (57 and 19).
16. Maldavsky, *Las crisis*, 37.
17. The title of Dostoevsky's novel as translated into Spanish is *El eterno marido*. Arlt's use of the expression here is presumably not coincidental?
18. Masotta, *El sexo*, 83.
19. Unmarried to each other, that is. Balder is estranged from his wife.
20. N. Berdyaev, *Solitude and Society* (London, 1938), 119.
21. Arlt was himself married twice, to Carmen Antinucci, who died, and just before his own death to Elizabeth Shine.
22. Masotta, *El sexo*, 77.
23. The tendency towards sociological jargon (*estructurada, espíritu grupal, individualizar, subtipos,*) is common in this work.
24. "¿Cuándo le dan el neumotórax?", asks one character of another in "Ester Primavera" [NCC III 247].
25. Jauretche, *El medio pelo*, 183.
26. Balder was a Norse god, of course, a further irony of Arlt's in choosing a heroic name for his most unheroic protagonist.
27. Núñez, *La obra*, 47, calls virginity in Arlt's work "el totem simbólico del valor femenino". Arlt himself writes: "La virginidad es para la mujer como un certificado de buena conducta" [NCC III 87].
28. Maldavsky, *Las crisis*, 75.
29. Núñez, *La obra narrativa*, 46.
30. Londres, *The Road*, 93.
31. Larra, *Roberto Arlt*, 121.
32. Etchenique, *Roberto Arlt*, 68.

CHAPTER IV

1. J. J. Gorini, "Arlt y los comunistas", *Contorno* no. 2 (May 1954), 8.
2. Gorini, p. 8.
3. J. J. Sebreli, "Inocencia...", 110.
4. Sebreli, 110.
5. Ghiano, *Constantes*, 99.
6. Masotta, *El sexo*, 11.
7. Goštautas places Arlt categorically, referring to "la literatura anarquista en lengua española, incluyendo autores como Baroja, Arlt y los escritores de Boedo", *Buenos Aires*, 247.
8. Quoted by Larra, *Roberto Arlt*, 45, from a newspaper article by Arlt which we have been unable to locate.
9. Etchenique, *Roberto Arlt*, 40.
10. Long known in English as *The Possessed*; in Spanish *Los endemoniados*. Arlt often refers to the Astrólogo as "el endemoniado". (See NCC II 93, for example.)
11. *The Devils*, 392.
12. Goštautas points out Arlt's liking for Andreyev, "el nihilista metafísico", *Buenos Aires*, 247. He fails to note that one of Andreyev's works is called *The Seven Hanged Men*. Perhaps even this title finds its parallel in *Los siete locos*?
13. *The Devils*, 422.
14. Quoted by Larra, *Roberto Arlt*, 54.
15. See James Joll, *The Anarchists* (London, 1964), 160. In general, however, anarchist philosophy is against technological advance. As Joll says: "When it comes to the point, the anarchists are all agreed that in the new society man will live in extreme simplicity and frugality and will be quite happy to do without the technical achievements of the industrial age" (277).
16. P. Orgambide, Introduction to the Hachette edition, *Nuevas aguafuertes porteñas* (1960), 11.
17. A. Pagés Larraya, "Buenos Aires en la novela", *Revista de la Universidad de Buenos Aires*, tercera época, tomo III, año IV, nos. 1-2 (1946), 253-75.
18. For a full treatment of this aspect of Arlt's work see J. M. Flint, "The Prose Style of Roberto Arlt", *Iberoamerikanisches Archiv*, (Berlin), no. 2 (1979), 161-77.

SELECT BIBLIOGRAPHY

1. *Prose Works by Arlt*

    (a) *First Editions*
    El juguete rabioso. Novel. Editorial Latina. Colección de autores
    noveles, 1926
    Los siete locos. Novel. Editorial Latina, 1929
    Los lanzallamas. Novel. Colección Claridad, 1931
    El amor brujo. Novel. Editorial Victoria, 1932
    El jorobadito. Short stories. Librería Anaconda
    El criador de gorilas. Short stories. (Published in *Hogar* and *El Mundo*,
    1935-36)
    Aguafuertes porteñas. Sketches. Editorial Victoria, 1933
    Aguafuertes españolas. Sketches. Talleres Gráficos Argentinos, 1936

    (b) *Subsequent Major Editions*
    Obras de Roberto Arlt. 8 Vols. Editorial Futuro, 1950-51
    Novelas completas y cuentos. 3 Vols. Fabril Editora, 1963
    Nuevas aguafuertes porteñas. Hachette, 1960

2. *Criticisms of Arlt's Prose Works*

    (a) *Books*
    Castellanos, Carmelina de, *Tres nombres en la novela argentina (Arlt,
    Mujica Lainez, Sábato)*, Rosario, 1967
    Etchenique, Nira, *Roberto Arlt*, Editorial La Mandrágora, 1962
    Goštautas, Stasys, *Buenos Aires y Arlt: (Dostoievski, Martínez Estrada
    y Escalabrini Ortiz)*, Insula, Madrid, 1977
    Gregorich, Luis, *La novela moderna: Roberto Arlt*, Fascículo no. 42
    of *Capítulo*, 1968, CEAL, 985-1008
    Guerrero, Diana, *Roberto Arlt: el habitante solitario*, Granica Editor,
    1972
    Hayes, Aden W., *Roberto Arlt: la estrategia de su ficción*, Támesis,
    London, 1981
    Larra, Raúl, *Roberto Arlt, el torturado*, Ediciones Alpe, 1956.
    (Amended, corrected and republished by Editorial Futuro,
    1950)
    Maldavsky, David, *Las crisis en la narrativa de Roberto Arlt*, Ed.
    Escuela, 1968

Masotta, Oscar, *Sexo y traición en Roberto Arlt*, Jorge Alvarez Editor, 1965

Núñez, Angel, *La obra narrativa de Roberto Arlt*, Editorial Nova, 1968

Pastor, Beatriz, *Roberto Arlt y la rebelión alienada*, Hispamérica, Gaithersburg, 1980

(b) *Selected Articles*

Anonymous, "Roberto Arlt sostiene que es de los escritores que van a quedar...", *La literatura argentina* (1929, núm.extraordinario), 25-27

Ara, G., *La incorporación de la realidad a la literatura argentina* (1964), 119

Arlt, M., "Recuerdos de mi padre", *Ficción* no. 15 (Sept.-Oct. 1958), 21-26

Arlt, M., Introduction to *Novelas completas y cuentos*, Fabril Editora (1963)

Barletta, L., "El juguete rabioso", *Nosotros*, Año XX, no. 211, 553-54

Bonet, C., *Historia de la literatura argentina*, Ed. Peuser (1959). Tomo IV, 218-20

Corelli, A. D., "El pensamiento rebelde de Roberto Arlt", *Universidad*, no. 70 (Santa Fe, Jan.-Mar. 1967), 49-60

Córdoba Iturburu, "Evocación de Roberto Arlt", *Cabalgata*, Part I "Los sueños y los personajes", Año I, no. 1 (Oct. 1946); Part II, "Autenticidad argentina en su literatura", Año I, no. 2 (Oct. 1946)

Cuneo, D., "Roberto Arlt: recuerdo" in *Aventura y letra de América*, Pleamar (1964), 188-90

Fernando, V., "Roberto Arlt", *Davar*, no. 22 (April 1949), 70-79

Flint, J. M., "Politics and Society in the Novels of Roberto Arlt", *Iberoamerikanisches Archiv*, II, no. 2 (Berlin, 1976), 155-63

Flint, J. M., "The Prose Style of Roberto Arlt", *Iberoamerikanisches Archiv*, V, no. 2 (Berlin, 1979), 161-77

García, G., *La novela argentina* (1952), 215-17

Goštautas, S., "Roberto Arlt, novelista de Buenos Aires", *Eco*, XXIV, nos. 141-42 (Bogotá, 1972), 238-73

Goštautas, S., "Vida y obra de Roberto Arlt", *Revista Nacional de Cultura*, XXXII, no. 204 (Caracas, 1972), 131-42

Goštautas, S., "La evasión de la ciudad en las novelas de Roberto Arlt", *Revista Iberoamericana*, XXXVIII, no. 80 (Pittsburgh, 1972), 441-62

Ghiano, J. C., "Los personajes de Roberto Arlt" in *Temas y aptitudes* (1949), 47-54